PRAISE FOR NAKED IN THE STREAM: ISLE ROYALE STORIES

"Eighteen tightly written stories that can be gripping at times and down right hilarious at others. You'll find out that there's more to Isle Royale than moose and wolf." Bill Castanier, Mittenlit.com

"...Witty and wonderful, humorous and dangerous, but always well told adventures." Konnie LeMay, *Lake Superior Magazine*

"The book introduces readers to several people who push themselves beyond conventional limits... For those who haven't visited or are unable to visit Isle Royale, *Naked in the Stream* is the best substitute you'll find." John Hogan, *The Grand Rapids Press*

"Besides Foerster's fine realistic nature descriptions and ability to build suspense, the book contains maps of Isle Royale and many wonderful illustrations by former Isle Royale Artist-in-residence, Joyce Koskenmaki. The entire compilation is an intimate look into what it means to find, revere and experience a wilderness." Tyler Tichelaar, *Marquette Monthly*

"If you liked Bill Bryson's A Walk in the Woods, you're going to love Naked in the Stream...these are tales told around a campfire after dark." Elizabeth Kane Buzzelli, *Northern Express Weekly*

"This is a lovely book. I'd put it in the can't-put-it-down category." Ray Nurmi, *Snowbound Books*, Marquette, MI

HIDDEN IN THE TREES

TREES

AN ISLE ROYALE SOJOURN

HIDDEN IN THE TREES

AN ISLE ROYALE SOJOURN

By

Vic Foerster

with Joyce Koskenmaki, Illustrator

Arbutus Press
Traverse City, MI

Hidden in the Trees: An Isle Royale Sojourn © 2017 Vic Foerster
ISBN 978-1-933926-23-0
Illustrations © 2017 Joyce Koskenmaki
Painting on cover, oil on linen, *Rauha* which means peace in Finnish.
© 2017 Joyce Koskenmaki
Maps © 2010, 2017 Michael Moore

Arbutus Press
Traverse City, Michigan
editor@arbutuspress.com
www.Arbutuspress.com

Library of Congress Cataloging-in-Publication Data

Names: Foerster, Vic, author. | Koskenmaki, Joyce, illustrator.
Title:Hidden in the trees :an Isle Royale sojourn/by Vic Foerster, with Joyce Koskenmaki, illustrator.
Other titles: Isle Royale sojourn
Description: Traverse City, Michigan : Arbutus Press, [2017] | Includes bibliographical references and index.
Identifiers: LCCN 2017018274 | ISBN 9781933926230 (alk. paper)
Subjects: LCSH: Isle Royale National Park (Mich.)--Description and travel. | Foerster, Vic--Travel--Michigan. | Trees--United States--Anecdotes. | Arborists--United States--Biography. | Nature conservation--United States.
Classification: LCC F572.I8 F67 2017 | DDC --dc23
LC record available at https://lccn.loc.gov/2017018274

Manufactured in the United States

CONTENTS

DEDICATION

Tim and Sue Bies,
Audrey Chamberlain,
Justin Plichta,
and Clay Hillman

And to friends everywhere who are willing to stand up for you.

ISLE
ROYALE

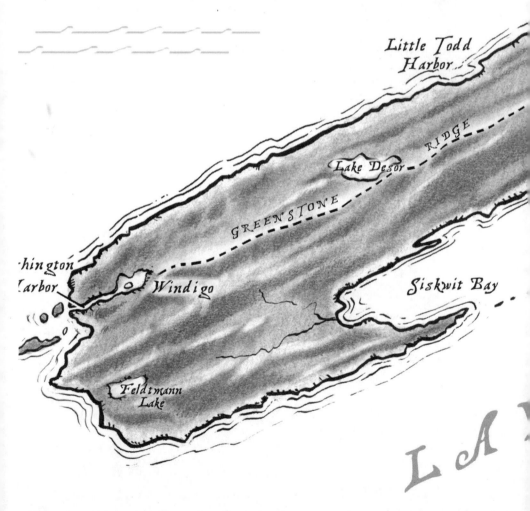

Little Todd
Harbor

RIDGE

GREENSTONE

Lake Desor

...hington
...arbor

Windigo

Siskwit Bay

Feldtmann
Lake

L A

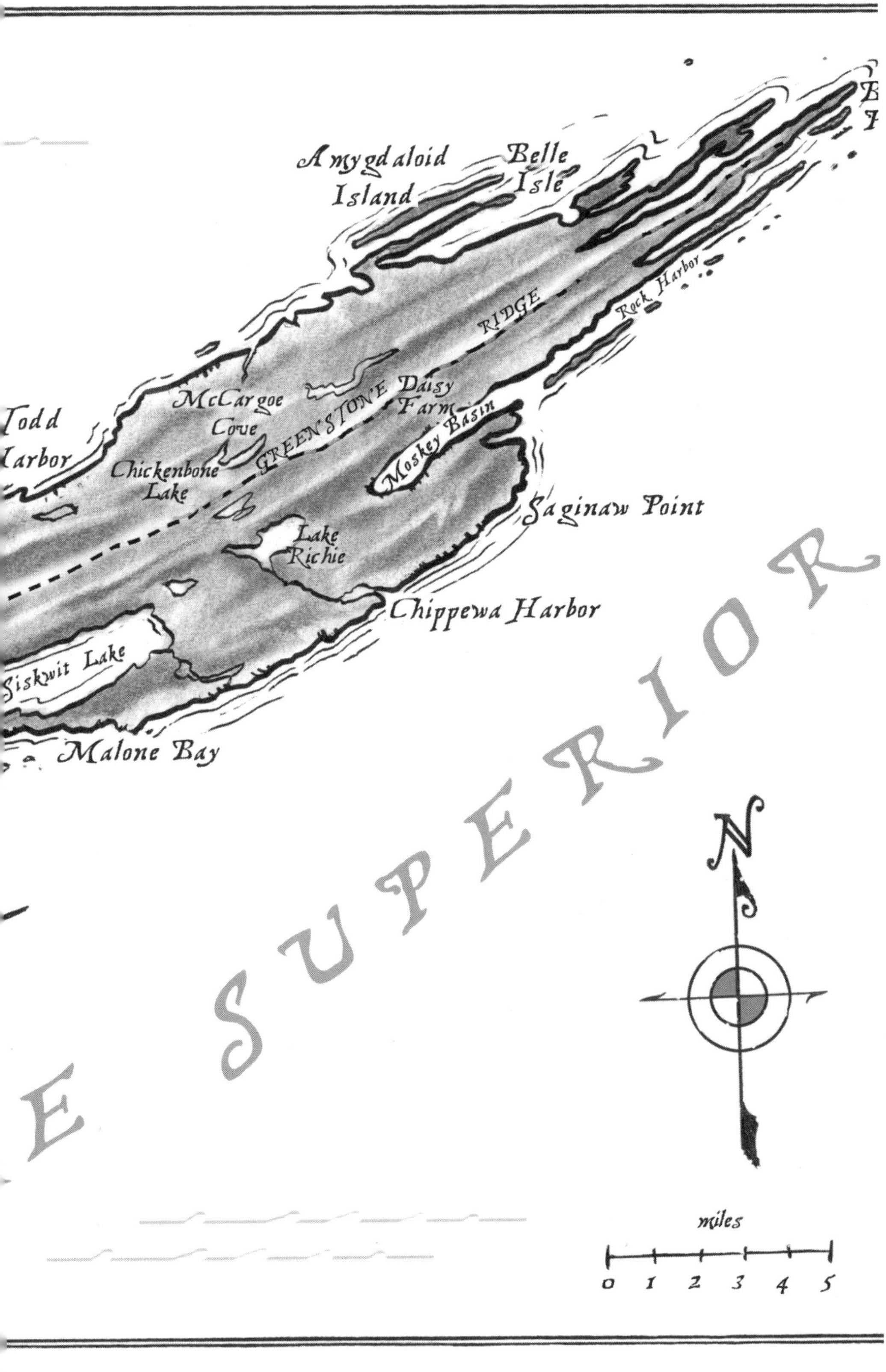

Amygdaloid
Island

Belle
Isle

B
7

RIDGE

Rock Harbor

Todd
Harbor

McCargoe
Cove

Daisy
Farm

GREENSTONE

Chickenbone
Lake

Moskey Basin

Saginaw Point

Lake
Richie

Chippewa Harbor

Siskwit Lake

Malone Bay

LAKE SUPERIOR

N

miles

0   1   2   3   4   5

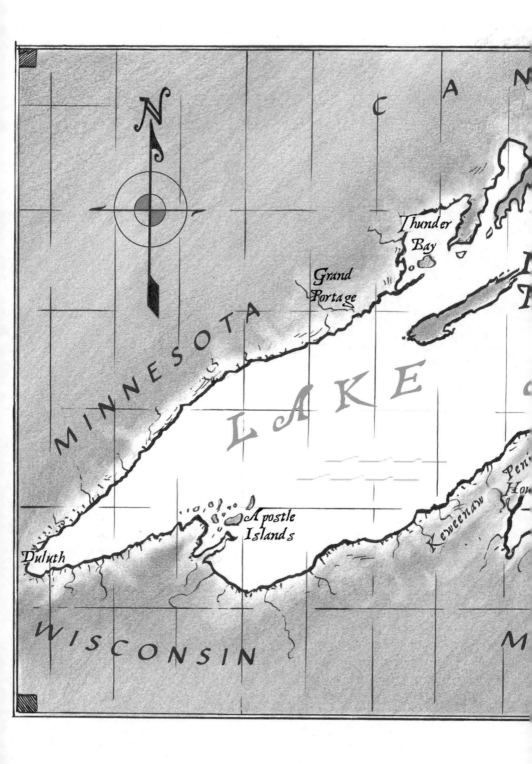

IN HER EYES

"I only went out for a walk, and finally concluded to stay out till sundown, for going out, I found, was really going in."

~John Muir

Sixteen months old, Natalie's young face is intent, almost rapt. This is her first spring, or the first one she's old enough to recognize as such. Released from both the upstairs flat where my son and his wife live and a winter-long containment, the new smells and sounds fascinate her. Mom and Dad wave from a third-floor window. They share the home with two other renters, one family to each of the home's three floors. Natalie smiles and waves back, then turns her attention to matters closer at hand.

Several neighbors greet us as we toddle down the sidewalk. It is early April and the trees haven't sprouted leaves yet, but the buds are swelling and the daffodils are showing promise of blooming. The robins are back in town and birdsong fills the thick spruce trees where they're busy nest building. Lawns are greening-up. People are outside in their yards raking up a winter's worth of debris. Joggers are breaking in their new shoes.

Natalie's a little unsteady on her feet, but more than up to the challenge of the short walk to the café located at the end of the street and across from the Madison City Zoo. At times, you can hear lions roar. You feel more than hear the growls as they reverberate through the thin walls of the kid's house, which certainly sounds exotic coming from an urban Wisconsin neighborhood.

Natalie is curious about everything we pass, repeating the single or double word answers I provide. She points at a person walking a dog, and I say, "Dog." She pats the trunk of a tree and I say, "Norway maple." I resist the urge to tell her the botanical name.

She suddenly let's go of my hand and clings to my leg.

"What's wrong?" I ask.

She's looking back the way we came as if scared.

15

Nobody is there. I gently ask again, "What is it?"

She glances up at me with an expression that can only be read as fear, but not fear as if she's terrified. It's as if she's concerned about an unknown. Is this a danger? At the same time, there's a hint of curiosity in her eyes, a question. I follow her gaze and notice that the light breeze is blowing a single oak leaf down the sidewalk. The lawns on either side of the pavement act like bumpers and the three-inch, raised turf prevents the leaf from escaping the walkway. There isn't quite enough wind to blow it over the lip of grass.

The leaf is following us.

It's a brown, brittle leftover from last fall. The leaf is dry and stiff. Each time a fresh gust nudges the leaf forward, its brittle edges scrape against the pavement, making a rasping sound. Natalie heard the quiet scrapes. It's a sound that I long ago learned to ignore but Natalie had turned to see who or what was following us.

I squeeze her hand, causing her to look up. I smile and quietly say, "It's okay," which slightly reassures her. I then reach down to see if she wants me to pick her up. She extends her arms to say yes and, once up, she wraps her arms around my neck. I have to pry them loose to breathe. We hurry a short distance down the sidewalk and then stop to see if the leaf follows. When the leaf catches up, we run a little farther and stop again. It quickly turns into a game. We eventually wait for the leaf to pass us. As it does, Natalie tenses slightly. I feel her breathe a sigh of relief when it finally climbs over the turf ahead of us and settle into a pile of its companions that have collected at the curb.

We walk the rest of the way to the café and step through the door. She wants down. I set her on her feet and she runs to the counter. Apparently, she has been here before. This is a world she understands.

Being outdoors delights young children. They often settle down when they feel the wind on their face. To a child, the natural world is a place of wonder, a place of discovery and joy. It's also a place of comfort. It's rare to see babies fussing when being pushed in a stroller, and once allowed outdoors, small children rarely beg to go back inside. One's first encounters with nature are often the most poignant, and Natalie's child-like sensitivity to her surroundings was something I'd hoped to regain while spending a self-imposed sabbatical on the wilderness island.

There was a time when curiosity and discovery drove scientists, when science focused more on enlightenment than on saving an endangered plant or rescuing an animal from extinction or calculating climate change. The men and women of science simply explored. The knowledge they gained resulted in…knowledge. To discover something new, a bird or an insect, was a big achievement. A scientist could be awarded an entire county in the New World for bringing home a species named after his or her king or queen.

Though I went to Isle Royale with few goals, I nevertheless accomplished a lot that month. I felt more refreshed, more alive. As a result, I now try to stay more in the moment. While I was there my senses did become more acute—almost Natalie-like. On the island, I took notice of wonders I often miss, and when I returned home, I sought books to further explore what I didn't understand. I sought out knowledgeable people. I would go so far as to say that I felt driven to understand what I'd seen: to try to understand how trees grow on bare rock, to relearn how scientists calculate the distance to stars (I'd forgotten), and why an insect moves his home from a spruce tree to a fir and back again.

Similar to Natalie, I often first reacted with fear when I was surprised by a moose on the trail. Moose are such huge animals. But the fear was quickly followed by, You're okay. If you leave them alone, they'll leave you alone. The adult in me made it nearly impossible to maintain a purely emotional reaction to such encounters. When I came upon a beaver dragging an aspen branch to its dam, I would marvel at his determination, then think, "Ah … good, he's improving a vital estuary."

I met many other park visitors during my stay, and they all have their own reasons for going to Isle Royale. Most, I noticed, also tend to take an objective, arm's-length view of nature. As adults, we seem to have a tendency to keep a professional distance. Campers would describe the weather in meteorological terms. Wildlife encounters were retold as if narrating a documentary. Many people brought guidebooks with them. After listening to them read aloud its contents, I began to wonder if they brought the books so they could better understand what they saw or if it was so they could be the first to identify the birds and plants. Apparently, among us "wilderness adventurers," there's a thinly veiled pride in being the first to identify the flora and fauna.

After spending a month on one of the most treasured—not to mention least visited—wilderness parks in North America, I think I better understand the reason we guard our emotions. I believe the arms-length approach to nature is a defense mechanism. Close encounters with the wild are too personal to talk freely about. They can be emotionally gripping moments. Whether witnessing the spectacle of a Northern Lights display, or being shocked at the swiftness with which a falcon sweeps a wren from the sky, or finding yourself scared stiff when a moose ambles by so close to you, you can see the moonlight glint off its black-globed eye—they are all, at their core, deeply intimate experiences.

I have the privilege of caring for the trees on some of the most beautiful and well-maintained estates in the Midwest. I can say with some authority that no expense is spared to care for those trees. The landscapes are as healthy and attractive as money can buy. I am fortunate to work at such places. With that said, I have come to realize that something vital is missing. After my time on Isle Royale, where the trees are maintained as wilderness, I see the plants I care for as specimens set in a zoo. The landscapes are replicas of native habitats. Often times, they're not even native.

I need to be careful how I say this for greening our communities, our city parks, and our homes is extremely important. Properly maintaining them is critical. Our trees contribute a tremendous amount of environmental and aesthetic benefits. They are benefits that improve the quality of our lives, and normally for the rest of the local flora and fauna as well. I don't mean to say that planting and maintaining trees and shrubbery and flowers and soils isn't important. It most certainly is. All I'm saying is that the current landscape—whether it's our own backyard, the community at large, or even the more rural woodlands, even the best ones—should not to be confused for being natural, and certainly not for wilderness. Most of the time, the land barely resembles what it once was.

No other plant better reflects conditions than trees do. In southern Michigan, where I normally make my living, the entire countryside has been altered to serve our purposes. There is no place left where the land isn't drastically changed. Gone entirely are the 200-foot trees that once forested the region.

John Muir, naturalist and advocate of the U.S. National Parks, defined wilderness as, "an area where the earth and its community of life are untrammeled by man, where man himself is a visitor who does not remain." Back in the 1930s, the founders of Isle Royale National Park used John Muir's definition as their guide. During the early planning phases for the park, serious consideration was given to razing all of the existing buildings, eliminating all trails and constructing no campgrounds. There was a contingent that felt that unless you break your own trail and make camp wherever you end the day, you are not traveling through real wilderness.

However, even back then and as isolated and remote as Isle Royale is, the majority of the park's founders realized that people couldn't be allowed to wander at will. They would soon destroy the fragile "ecosystem," a word not yet in their vocabulary. To re-create as true a wilderness as possible—for Isle Royale had been mined and logged during the 19th century and early 20th—the early planners reached a compromise with those who wanted a trail-less park. The planners decided to build a few scattered campgrounds and connect them with paths. They called these paths "twelve-inch man-ways." They were a first for the National Park Service. Until that time, all national park trails had been the size of small roads or lanes and access to motor vehicles was encouraged.

To this day, the trails on Isle Royale remain no more than narrow paths that wind through the woods and hills. In many places, they are difficult to distinguish from game trails. I think Mr. Muir would have approved of the compromise.

*

The walk to the café with Natalie caused me to recall my trip to Isle Royale. Her riveted attention to a single leaf reminded me that I not only needed time to get away, I needed to find a place where I felt the urge to explore again, to notice things, to grow curious. I had become so efficient at filtering out all of the degradation to the land that I had quit asking questions. My filter had grown so dark, so thick, that I was in danger of losing interest altogether.

Natalie's fear of a single leaf caused her to grow silent and cling to my leg. She never whimpered or cried out. Did some long-lost danger-instinct spring to life that made her go silent, as a fawn does when threatened? When we left the café, I picked up a leaf and gave it to her. In retaliation for being frightened, I thought she might crumple it in her tiny fist. Instead, she grasped the leaf and wanted to take it home to show Mom and Dad.

On the walk home, we stopped to watch leaves blow down the street so she could listen to the sounds they make. The wind was in our faces now, and, although quite cold, it did not cause her to cower or want to hurry indoors. In fact, she never made the slightest complaint until I said, "It's time to go inside."

AN ACT OF GOD

"If you are seeking ideas, go out walking.
Angels whisper to a man when he goes for a walk."

~Raymond Inmon

THE PATH FROM CHICKENBONE LAKE TO McCARGO COVE IS FAIRLY FLAT. THAT DOESN'T mean it's smooth. The path changes pitch with each step and, like all of the trails on Isle Royale, it's laced with countless surface roots and rocks. I stumble more than I care to admit when hiking here, and tripping and falling is something to avoid, especially when portaging a canoe or toting a heavy pack. Medical help is a day away or more. I'm careful to watch my feet with each step I take.

This evening's hike, however, is different. It's a light one. I am carrying only a fishing pole and some tackle. It's literally a walk in the park. I'm returning to camp at the end of the day with a nice catch of walleye, and eager to get back and cook them up for dinner. Early tomorrow morning, I'll return to Chickenbone Lake to fish again, so I am leaving the canoe behind. The pack-less, canoe-less hike allows me the luxury of looking up—with only an occasional glance at my feet. I like the idea that I can walk with my head up and see what's happening around me. When I'm home, I tend to overlook what surrounds me, and I worry that life is passing me by unnoticed. My focus on my day-to-day duties often consumes me. I sure don't want to behave that way here, not now. For once, I want to see the world with eyes wide-open, especially this world.

Yet, for all of my ambition to see the island, I feel strangely uncomfortable. It's not normal to walk anywhere on Isle Royale without carrying something heavy: firewood, a backpack, the canoe. So instead of totally enjoying the walk back to camp, I find myself involuntarily looking over my shoulder to see if I dropped something. And it's more than the load-less, casual stroll that makes me anxious.

The canoe likes to wander.

In the past, I've seen a wave's surge lift the canoe off the shore and float her onto the lake. In the middle of the night, a sudden gust of wind blows her off the beach. Other times, during the split-second I've turned my back to locate the next pack to stow, the canoe has silently floated away, making tracks for open water. More than once I've had to wade into frigid water to retrieve her. Not once has she cried out in warning. It's as if she wants to sneak away—to rendezvous with some other boat or see what the kayaks are up to.

It would be foolish to lug the heavy watercraft all the way to camp and carry it all the way back in the morning. The canoe weighs 70 pounds. Camp is a mile away. That kind of labor-saving logic normally cures my most unreasonable of fears. But this time it doesn't. So, I made a compromise with her. She can stay at the lake, but only if she promises to stay where I left her, dragged 30 feet from the water's edge and lashed to a tree. I hide the paddles down the trail where she can't find them.

Where the canoe chafes on her leash, Chickenbone Lake is so shallow that it's more of a marsh than lake. Downstream, the marsh feeds a small creek that parallels the trail I'm hiking. Both the trail and the creek will eventually find their way to McCargo Cove across from the campground where I'm staying. The creek is supplemented by several other rivulets and washes along the way. At first, the creek barely moves. Thick vegetation, rocks and forest debris hinder the water's progress and cause it to back up into swampy pools. At its headwaters, the creek seeps more than flows. One mile later, that seep has turned into a 20-foot-wide stream that's two-to-three-feet deep. The current is strong enough to bend the pike-reeds growing in the delta.

Right beside the trail, and halfway to camp, I pass a lone 80-foot tall white pine. The pine stands as straight as a utility pole. It has no official name, but I call it, "halfway pine." Its poker-straight, slender trunk testifies to its valley-bottom protection from the wind. Dangling from the bottom limb of the pine is a broken branch that hangs directly over the path. I first noticed the dangling branch 25 years ago, during one of my earliest trips to the island. Evidently, one of the upper branches in the pine either snapped in a storm or cracked under a heavy snow-load and caught its fall in the tree's lowest limb, which is still forty feet high.

Over the years, I've studied the dangling branch with a sort of professional curiosity. The broken branch forks into two smaller branches, forming a wishbone. The two forks of the wishbone point ground-ward. The falling branch must have landed so perfectly on top of the limb that it came to rest in the crook of the wishbone. That had to be a neat trick, something I wish I could have been here to witness. In stiff winds, the branch rocks back and forth in its cradle. If the wind is strong enough, the branch rocks so hard that coming down the trail, you can hear that cradle creak before you see it.

The wishbone arms are too long for the wind to flip the branch off the limb, so as long as the wood remains sound, there's no chance it will blow from its perch. I use this path almost every year and each season I hold my breath approaching Halfway Pine. I expect the branch to have finally decayed enough to snap and fall. I picture the branch landing atop some unsuspecting hiker, the unlucky person lying in the middle of the trail knocked-out cold. That's highly unlikely given the few people who pass this way. But, similar to my concerns for my wayward canoe, I have good reason to worry about falling branches.

It is obvious that branches fall, and they must fall all the time. There's ample evidence of it given the number of limbs on the ground. The forest floor is covered with them. You can barely take more than ten steps through the woods without having to step over a limb or fallen tree. And yet, it is rare to see a branch fall. The trees must be shy about it. For as an arborist, I'm practically always looking up at them. You'd think I would catch them dropping their limbs. Seeing that branch just hang there, year-after-year, poised to join his fallen cousins, I can't help but ask, "Are you waiting for me to walk beneath you?"

I do have good reason to be concerned. A few years earlier, on a windless mid-summer day, a young couple was walking down a Kalamazoo city street. The husband was walking 10 feet ahead of his wife. Overhead, they heard a loud crack and felt a rush of wind. The wife watched in horror as a large limb fell from an old cherry tree and crushed her husband just as he looked up. He died four days later.

The family's loss of income, not to mention the terrible personal loss, was beyond calculation. The medical bills were astronomical. Thinking the old cherry tree belonged to the city, since it was located in the parkway beside the street, the wife hired an attorney to sue the city for negligence for not pruning off the decrepit old limb.

Her attorney, Mr. James Mahoney, discovered during his investigation that the tree was not on city property but actually belonged to the homeowner. The easement for that particular street was only fifty feet wide, not the normal sixty-six. That placed the cherry tree two inches outside of the right-of-way. During his research, Mr. Mahoney also learned from a neighbor that a limb had fallen from the same tree a couple of years earlier, crushing the neighbor's fence. Believing that the previous incident, coupled with the recent tragedy, confirmed the negligence charge, Mr. Mahoney pressed charges against the property owners to cover the medical bills and loss of income. The property owners denied responsibility and the whole matter headed to court.

Mr. Mahoney hired me to do a forensic exam of the cherry tree. The property owners were a couple who had lived in the house for 10 years. They hired their own attorney, a Mr. Alfred Townsend, to represent them. For reasons that were never made clear, the homeowner's insurance policy didn't cover the accident and the insurance company was never involved.

Mr. Townsend's clients wouldn't allow me access to the cherry tree without his presence. So, with both attorneys, the homeowners, and several neighbors watching, I examined the tree that killed the pedestrian.

I don't normally draw an audience when I do my job, and confess I felt a certain amount of pride that my role was considered important enough to watch. It also made me self-conscious. Mr. Mahoney instructed me not to say anything to the other side or to the neighbors. He had already shown me photographs of the accident scene, close-ups of where the limb ripped out of the tree, and pictures taken from several different angles of the fatal limb lying in the street. The photos of the accident scene showed leaves and twigs scattered across the ground. I could see some dried blood on the pavement. Mr. Mahoney provided me the police reports that contained interviews of the neighbors, the homeowners, and the emotionally-wrought comments from the victim's wife.

It can be difficult, but at moments like these I try to stay focused on the tree. It is easy to become emotionally involved, to sympathize for the family and lose objectivity, which can prove disastrous for the client I'm trying to help. If the defense can poke holes in my assessment or say I'm biased, my work could be counterproductive. Attorneys have advised me to stick to the facts. Victims are to be described as a "35-year-old Caucasian male" or injuries expressed as "a clean cut, 3-inches deep, 6-inches wide." They tell me to avoid adjectives.

This tree was a black cherry, *Prunus serotina*. Black cherries can go by several common names—chokecherry, black cherry or wild cherry. They can grow to 120 feet tall and are highly valued for their wood, though not their fruit as the cherries are extremely bitter. This was a big tree. It had a trunk diameter of 52 inches. The tree's crown covered two entire front yards and extended well over the street.

At 12 feet high, the main trunk divided into a whorl of six large limbs. Each limb was 12 to 24 inches in diameter. All six were connected to the tree as if from the hub of a wheel, which is a highly unusual configuration for a black cherry. Ordinarily, they grow a single, main stem with each limb branching off every two to six feet. Evidently, when this tree was young, the top had snapped, causing the tightly-packed limbs to grow at one focal point.

Climbing a short ladder, I examined the trunk of the tree where the fatal limb had broken away. There was only a narrow band of healthy, green-wood located at the bottom of the prior attachment. The rest of the wood was soft and punky, or absent altogether.

The foliage throughout the entire tree was a pale green, not the deep green that healthy cherry trees have in June. There was a great deal of dieback in the upper third of the tree's crown—all clear indications of a tree in decline. There was also a large hole on the northwest side of the main trunk, located four feet off the ground. When I stuck my head inside the hole (it was that big) and examined it with a flashlight, the cavity ran out of sight up the tree.

I put the ladder back in the truck and grabbed my camera. I took several pictures, snapping shots from all sides and from varying distances. I had to work my way across the adjacent yards, trying to avoid conversations with the neighbors without seeming rude. I also photographed other trees on the street. I noted there were only two other cherry trees. The rest of the street trees were silver maples and red oaks, and they were several years younger than the cherries.

As I clicked the last photo, I told Mr. Mahoney I was done and picked up my tools. He walked over to Mr. Townsend and they had a brief conversation that I couldn't hear. When finished, he returned and told me he'd call me tomorrow.

On the phone the next day, I informed Mr. Mahoney the tree was obviously in rough condition and I felt the homeowner ought to have seen it was dangerous. Given its history of dropping limbs, its overall poor condition, and its location directly over two driveways, the sidewalk and the road, I said, "If this isn't a case of neglect, then I don't know what is. If this tree belonged to the city, they'd be trying to settle as we speak."

Mr. Mahoney told me, chances are good that Mr. Townsend will want to depose you. He'll want to know what you will say to the judge before this goes to trial. I'll call you when he does.

✳

On Isle Royale, where the creek flows past Halfway Pine, there's enough current to hear the water flow. The creek spills along its water-course over the same sort of tree roots and rocks that cause me to stumble when hiking. The water stumbles over obstructions more gracefully than I do—splashing along in a series of gentle drips, tinkles, gurgles and plinks. The creek's constant flow is a continual water source for Halfway Pine.

My landmark pine turns all of that sweet-sounding water into pine sap, that same sticky, gooey substance that is so hard to clean off cars or patio furniture. How such a thick material flows through solid wood is a mystery—even for an arborist. For in addition to the wood cell's resistance, the sap is defying gravity. Mysteriously, only live trees can draw, suck, seep, move and transport water as high as a 25-story building.

Capillary action plays a part in powering sap flow, but just a little. Capillary action is what causes liquids to creep across a solid surface. It is strong enough to draw blood up eight-inch capillary tubes, but not up a 150-foot tree.

Respiration also plays a role. Leaves breathe, as do pine needles. Their breathing, or transpiration as it's called, acts as a weak pump. The loss of moisture through the stomata of thousands of needles creates a vacuum that needs to be filled. But trees aren't bundles of hollow wooden tubes. Transpiration alone isn't strong enough to pull water through all of the membranes of the wood cells that lie between root tip and branch tip.

Another issue with respiration being strong enough to transport all of that tree sap is that even dormant trees transport sap, and lots of it. Sugar maples are an example of that. They are tapped for maple syrup when they have no leaves. The ground is often frozen. It's why the sap is sweet. The maple hasn't yet been infused with enough soil compounds to spoil the taste. It's pure tree sap, and if tapped at the right time of year, maple syrup producers say a good-size tree will supply up to 3.2 gallons of sap per day.

Trees that are pruned in late winter will drip sap from their wounds. On sugar maples, the drips form a sweet tasting icicle. The drips from sassafras taste like root beer. I receive several calls each February concerning the so-called "bleeding" from pruning cuts. The concern is, "Will my tree bleed to death?" or "Does it hurt the tree?" The answer to both is no. Trees not only don't bleed to death, but the loss of sap doesn't faze them. Trees don't leak. The sap is replaced in dormant trees as fast as it's lost.

Botanists say the most plausible explanation for what powers sap flow is that trees create an internal osmotic pressure. When powered by photosynthesis, leaves increase the sugar levels in the tree's crown, which creates a sugar imbalance. As a result, the tree moves sap around to reach an equilibrium. During the dormant season, without the aid of photosynthesis, the tree creates a sugar imbalance by triggering a hormonal surge at the buds and/or roots. The tree, more or less, tricks itself to transport sap.

If you cut down a tree in the spring, the sap flow is typically so strong that the woodcutter will get soaked, and not in sweat. Strike a soft-wooded tree like a cottonwood or sycamore with an ax, and they splash you. In the spring, there is so much water pressure within a tree that arborists can't use trunk injections, which are an arborist's version of an intra-venous drip. The pressure is so great it spits the tubes out.

One cold February night in Grand Rapids, when temperatures dropped to a minus 28° Fahrenheit, the older sycamores in town literally exploded. The frozen sap had expanded to a point where the trunks burst. Driving to work that morning, I couldn't help but rubber neck at the gaping fissures. The splits were so wide that even driving at 35 miles per hour, I could see completely through 30-inch diameter trees. Calls flooded into the office. When temperatures warmed to a comparable balmy 15° by afternoon, the fissures snapped shut. It sounded like gunfire. After the splits closed, I could only detect a barely perceptible seam running up and down the bark to indicate the trauma that had occurred. I still drive by many of these trees. They all survived, and as if nothing ever happened to them.

The water pressure required to transport sap up Halfway Pine is created by a blend of capillary action, osmotic pressure, respiration, enzyme triggers and unknown factors. The proper mix of all of these remains unknown and is a set of conditions that scientists are unable to recreate.

What's so puzzling about the process, of course, is that not only does the sap flow straight up, but it passes through what appears to be solid wood, and it fights gravity the whole way.

And gravity is relentless. Lugging canoes and packs on uneven trails makes me feel like an authority on gravity. I sweat. My feet end up sore, my soles grow hot. If I don't sit down soon, blisters aren't far behind. It's all that pressure. Gravity causes pressure and pressure causes heat. What I don't understand is, if my feet grow warm from only lugging a 50 - pound pack, why then isn't the base of a tree warm? With the tons of wood that sit atop a standing tree, why wouldn't the incredible pressure cause the stump to grow so hot it bursts into flames?

*

It was three months before I heard from Mr. Mahoney. He said the deposition had been scheduled. Depositions are sort of a pre-trial. There's no judge or jury, just a legal recorder who transcribes everything said. Depositions are used by attorneys to discover what witnesses will testify to. Depositions help to avoid unwanted surprises in the courtroom and often result in a settlement, which also avoids wasting the court's valuable time.

Mr. Mahoney wanted me to meet with him prior to the deposition for some last-minute instructions, which proved fortunate. I'd been taught to answer opposing attorney's questions truthfully, of course, but as briefly as possible, volunteering no additional information. Mr. Mahoney, however, instructed me to expound on why I thought the tree was a hazard and why a homeowner should have seen the danger and done something about it.

"We're trying to convince the judge this case merits a hearing," he told me. "Judges are supposed to read all of the deposition transcripts. They're a very important part of the process." Shuffling some papers on the lunch-counter where we were meeting, he told me, "The other side will avoid asking you questions that offer you an opportunity to lend credence to our claim of negligence. I am not allowed to ask you any questions. I'm just there to object if he gets out of line. To circumvent his tactics, I need you to fill in the blanks he's trying to leave void."

This was a new approach and I liked it. For once, I could speak more freely.

The proceedings were to be held at Mr. Townsend's office. When we arrived there, the receptionist paged him. He came right out, shook our hands and thanked us for being on time. Both attorneys wore suits and ties, and carried it off so naturally that it was as if they wore jeans and a T-shirt. How that's possible I will never understand. Nobody wears a tie at the tree service.

Mr. Townsend led us to a conference room. The room had no windows, which always makes me feel uncomfortable. There were a few brass-framed, glass-covered photographs of famous skylines—New York, Tokyo, London. In the center of the room was an oval, walnut-veneered table with evenly-spaced high-backed metal chairs. He directed us to the chairs, asked if we wanted any water, and said he'd be right back with the recorder.

"Kind of sterile," I said to Mr. Mahoney, who was taking documents out of his briefcase.

"Yes, these places aren't designed to make you feel at home. At least the room isn't so small. The last deposition I …" He was interrupted by Mr. Townsend's return.

The recorder walked in behind him. Her name was Grace, and she was a professional-looking woman, dressed in gray slacks and a white, high-buttoned blouse worn beneath a navy blazer. She looked to be in her 40s. She asked me to raise my right hand and she swore me in. She reminded me that all of my answers must be verbalized. Nods or shrugs could not be recorded into the transcript. When the instructions were completed, she asked everyone present to say and spell their full names.

We did.

Turning to Mr. Townsend, Grace said, "We're ready."

He turned in his swivel chair to face me, and smiled. "Are you comfortable, Mr. Foerster? And may I call you Vic during these proceedings?"

I answered, "Yes, and I'm as comfortable as can be expected. Thank you."

"All right. Vic … Before we begin, I want to express to you, and Mr. Mahoney, how terrible my clients feel about all of this … for the family. This is a tragic accident. My clients want the family to understand they are only trying to protect themselves from being wrongfully blamed." He paused to allow this to sink in.

We nodded. I didn't doubt they felt bad.

Mr. Townsend asked if I knew any of the people involved prior to being contacted by Mr. Mahoney. I hadn't. He then asked for my credentials. I told him my educational background, gave a brief work history, and filled in some details on prior cases I'd testified at.

"Vic, we will begin by my showing you a series of photographs that have been entered into evidence." He pulled a manila folder out of his briefcase that contained a stack of 8½ x 11 photographs. Mr. Mahoney leaned over to see if they were the same pictures he had.

"Please take a look at the photograph in exhibit D-4 and tell me, if in your opinion, whether you believe an ordinary citizen would realize this tree poses an immediate risk to a passerby."

I thought, so this is where he's going. The photograph was of the cherry tree where the six tightly packed limbs attached to the trunk. Remembering my instructions, I said, "This is a very unusual and old black cherry. Normally, the main limbs on cherries don't grow so close together. This tight configuration definitely weakens their connection to the main trunk."

"But would a layman know that?"

"Not likely," I admitted.

Mr. Mahoney squirmed a little in his seat.

"Vic," Mr. Townsend continued, "please examine the photos in what's summarized as exhibit D-7. Please tell me whether an ordinary citizen would think the limb in these pictures is a hazard." Mr. Townsend pointed to one of the still remaining six limbs attached to the tree in exhibit D-7a.

Studying the photo, I said, "See how there's no branch collar? No bulge where the limb attaches to the tree? The limb looks like a pipe that's poked straight into the trunk—not a good sign. Notice the dark stains beneath the limb from where sap oozes from cracks and fissures. These are all clear signs of a weak limb attachment." Spinning the photograph to face Mr. Townsend, I pointed to the stains.

Grace broke in and said, "Please say aloud what you are pointing at."

I did so.

Pointing to a different limb, I said. "When you look at this other limb, third one from the right in Exhibit D-7c, the branch collar is prominent. The bulge where the limb connects to the trunk is large. The bark is clean and healthy looking, no stains. Exhibits D-7 show good examples of the differences between a weak attachment and a strong one …"

Mr. Townsend broke in, "Is that something a homeowner would necessarily know?"

"That's difficult to say." I hesitated. "I'd think someone who's lived in a home for any length of time would look pretty hard at this tree. Given its age and location over the road and sidewalk, they should question its health. I'm told another limb besides the one that killed the victim recently fell from this tree. That should do more than raise an eyebrow, even for a layman."

"Mr. Foerster … sorry, Vic, please study these close-ups from where the fatal limb broke out of the tree and also look at this second picture of the limb lying in the street." Mr. Townsend pushed the two photographs across the conference table and positioned them for a clearer view. Pointing to the limbs in question, he said, "In the first photo, note the condition of the wood where the limb was connected to the tree. Now, in the second photograph, note the condition of the trunk where the limb broke away. It appears to me, though I fully admit I'm no tree expert, that the connection on the underside of this limb, the fatal limb, and the only side one could see from the ground, appears normal, appears healthy-looking if you will. Is that how it appears to you?"

I studied both photographs for almost a full minute. I was stalling. I'd already noticed the sound wood on the underside of the fallen limb when I did the site inspection. The bottom-side of the limb looked strong because it was strong. It was the rest of the wood that was rotten. The other three sides and the interior of the fallen limb—the top, left and right sides—would be difficult, if not impossible, to see from the ground.

I cleared my throat and said, "Mr. Townsend, you will note the rot and decay. Ninety percent of the wood is decayed or absent altogether. It's clearly rotten."

"But the question is could that be detected from the ground?"

I swallowed hard. "If you only looked at this limb from the ground or if you never had the tree examined by an arborist, or, say, only gave it a casual glance, it is unlikely a person—a layperson—would spot all of that decay. However, it is my opinion, given the tree's overall poor condition and its history, that this tree should have raised serious questions for the homeowner."

As an afterthought, I then added, "My wife would have been concerned. She would have called someone." I winced. *Oh, bad example. Of course an arborist's wife would notice a hazard tree in her yard. And my wife would not appreciate me mentioning her. God help me if they ask her to testify.*

Fortunately, Mr. Townsend didn't pursue it.

Taking a different tact, Mr. Townsend asked, "Vic, if this tree had been inspected by an arborist, even a certified arborist, would they have been able to determine that the fatal limb posed a risk?"

"Yes, a certified arborist would have certainly detected the danger."

"But ... would a certified arborist have detected it from the ground? When you are called to inspect trees, to do 'tree-risk-assessments' as you arborists like to call them, do you normally get off the ground to inspect trees?"

The question caught me by surprise and I hesitated again. I'd never been asked that before. "Well ... I only climb trees when I think there's reason to," I finally answered. "But I honestly believe I would have in this case—if I'd been called prior to the accident."

"Has it been your experience that most arborists climb trees to do tree-risk-assessments?"

"I couldn't say what *most* arborists do, Mr. Townsend."

"You don't want to venture an opinion—an expert opinion—on the matter?"

"No, I don't."

He's good, I thought. If pressed, I'd have to say that I rarely climb trees to do inspections.

"One last photograph. Please look at this photo of the street. This looks to me like any other tree-lined street in town. Do you really think people would stop walking down this road because they're scared that trees are going to fall on their heads? If anything, I think the trees invite a person for a stroll."

Nicely put, I thought. *But, he just helped our cause.* "Mr. Townsend, this photograph clearly shows how bad the cherry tree is compared to the rest of the trees on the street. Look at that sparse, half-dead top. It really stands out. The other trees—mostly younger maples and oaks—are full, the leaves a deeper green color. There's barely any dieback."

Mr. Townsend put the photographs away, paused as if trying to remember if he had any other questions to ask, and finally said, "I believe we're finished here. Thank you for your time, Mr. Foerster." He stood up to shake my hand and gave me the same smile as when he'd opened his questioning, a hard-to-read smile.

Did he think he'd achieved his purpose? Was he actually happy to work with me? It didn't seem likely.

Outside in the parking lot, I asked Mr. Mahoney how I did.

The question seemed to surprise him. "Good," he said. "You handled yourself professionally, tried to fill in the blanks. It's pretty obvious where he wants to take this. Chances are good that nothing more will happen until after the judge reads the transcripts and studies the documents. It could be six months before you hear back from me. Be prepared to go to trial. I believe we have a strong case."

It was almost a year before I heard from Mr. Mahoney. The year had flown by. At the tree service, we'd been swamped with work. An April storm with winds clocked at 80 miles per hour ripped through several of the older neighborhoods in town. The damage was so severe that entire trees toppled over. The city looked like a war zone for a couple of weeks until the debris was cleaned up and power restored. The straight-line winds, as the meteorologists called them, lasted for only 10 minutes. But the Chinook express of cold air being exchanged for warm left a wake of destruction that created a six-month backlog of tree pruning and removals.

When Mr. Mahoney called, he caught me off-guard. Bent over my desk, preoccupied with writing a lengthy pruning estimate for Oakwood Estates, a development that needed to be renamed, it took a second to remember who he was.

Punching the blinking button on the desk phone, I said, "Mr. Mahoney, it's been a while. How are you doing? What's happening with our case?"

"I'm fine, Vic. Thanks for asking. I've been meaning to call you. Just been busy is all. Sorry about not getting back to you. The case was settled two months ago."

"Settled?"

"Yes. Well, sort of." He hesitated before saying, "Vic, the judge tossed it out. He said the case had no merit."

Surprised, I asked, "How can that be?"

"The judge called the accident 'An Act of God.' She ruled that a falling limb is no different than somebody dying in a hurricane or a flood or any other natural disaster. She didn't buy the neglect charge at all."

Trying to wrap my head around the judge's decision, I asked, "An Act of God? Is that really a legal term? Did the ruling actually read, 'God killed him?'"

"Not in those words, of course, but I'm afraid so. It's an ancient legal expression. The phrase goes way back in case law, to the Greeks, in fact."

I took a deep breath. "Oh man, what will the wife do? Will she get any assistance at all?"

"I'm afraid not. They had no insurance. He was laid off and she works a part-time retail job."

Mr. Mahoney said he had a call on another line and thanked me for my services, and said he'd call if he needed me in the future. We said our goodbyes.

After hanging up, I leaned back in the chair and stared out the window. Did I say something wrong? Were Mr. Mahoney's documents poorly written? Did I miss something pertinent?

A light breeze ruffled the leaves in the silver maple outside the office window, causing the leaves to flip over and reveal their bright undersides. No insurance, little income. I can't imagine what her medical bills must be. Somebody should have stepped in and helped. What's homeowner's insurance for if it won't handle accidents like this?

The city certainly could have done more. At least a third of that tree hung over the street. Didn't they bear any responsibility?

"An Act of God?"

Shaking my head, I went downstairs and poured a cup of coffee, wishing it was something stronger.

✳

Every living tree battles gravity. The struggle causes no heat, and if you place an ear against a tree trunk, you hear no bubbles or gurgles, no gushing or groans.

As a gag gift, I once received a "tree" stethoscope for a birthday gift. In jest, I have been asked by a handful of clients if I carry one in my toolbox. No need. Trees are silent (though I admit I tried it once when I was alone). Trees may creak in the wind. The leaves may rustle. But there's no audible indication of the stress taking place within them—until they fall.

Then it can be epic. When gravity finally wins, an old oak strikes the ground with the force of a million sledge hammers. The ground trembles. But for all of its mighty wallop, the oak's fall causes the ground to tremble for only a second or two. And when that ancient oak or pine or walnut finally grows still, their struggle with gravity is over.

Some of the most dramatic, and tragic tree accidents, occur on dead-calm days during extended periods of drought, and with no warning. A limb drops, crushing whatever or whoever lies below. During tornados, it's no surprise that trees are ripped from the ground. We expect limbs to snap in high winds. But why does a tree wait until a calm summer day to inexplicably fall?

I didn't buy the Act of God decision—be it a legally accepted excuse or not. I blame gravity as opposed to the Almighty. This arborist's best guess is that gravity finally won its battle with that cherry limb. The sap slowed to a crawl. The wood became weak and the tree simply lost its grip. The timing could not have been worse.

Admittedly, it wasn't the first time I'd been involved in a tree-related fatality, or gone to court over it, and it's not that I haven't had other occasions to blame God for misfortune or ask why He allows these terrible accidents to occur. There was a time when I used to try to find nice, neat spiritual explanations for why trees kill people. And I have asked God, as I suspect most people have, why He allows drunk drivers or cancer or disease to remove mothers from their children. It's one of those personal questions that at some point cause us to point a finger skyward and demand an answer.

Attempting to find some answers, I've read books on the subject by authors I respect. I've read and reread the book of Job. I've listened to a few preachers who dared to broach the subject from the pulpit. I still couldn't help but ask the unfair question of what was wrong with that person that they paid such a heavy price? It was nothing I could see.

I've reached the point where I shake my head at the news of such awful losses. But instead of looking for blame, I now help where I can and lend a shoulder to cry on if possible. And despite my unanswered questions, I say a prayer for the family and … think of my father.

I had a half-brother who died when I was only two. His name was Charles Edward Foerster III and he was only eight when he passed away. I have no memory of him, and am told they called him Chuckles since my great-grandfather's name was Charles, my grandfather's name was Charles, and my Dad was, also. To clarify who each Charles was, the family called my father's son, Chuckles. They called my father, Chuck or Buzz, and called my grandfather Carl. Chuckles is the only child of Dad's first marriage, and he was born with cystic fibrosis. The disease is hereditary and occurs when the "right" two people who carry the gene come together. Not all children of such couples acquire the disease, but chances are close to 25 percent. At the time, the disease was always fatal.

I never asked Dad, but I believe he and his first wife decided not to have any more children. Contraceptives being what they were in the 1940s and sterilization carrying strong negative connotations, birth control for them had to be an awkward affair. They were high school sweethearts and had married young. The marriage didn't last.

Currently, life expectancy for cystic fibrosis patients is closer to 40 years, sometimes longer. But in the 1940s, most children with cystic fibrosis died by the time they reached the age of 12. Surely, during my brother's eight short years, Dad and his first wife must have felt a horrific clock ticking.

I didn't ask my Dad if he was bitter about the loss of Chuckles until near the end of Dad's life. My Mother was already gone. Dad and I were standing outside on the deck grilling burgers. He was telling me how proud he was that my younger brother, Dave, worked for a Christian mission organization in Southeast Asia, and how thrilled he was that my youngest son, Nick, is a youth pastor for a church in Wisconsin. Dad seemed deeply moved.

Dad clearly loved God and, frankly, I didn't know exactly why. Growing up, my parents rarely took us to church. We seldom said grace or did many of those activities I'd normally associate with Christians. Both my Mom and Dad told us they believed in God. Still, we were not what I thought of as a religious family. I finally got up enough nerve to ask him why we seldom went to church as kids. Was it maybe because he was bitter about losing Chuckles?

I could immediately tell I'd hurt him. Lowering his voice, he quietly said, "No, we mostly didn't go because we just got out of the habit." He didn't say any more.

I felt terrible for asking and changed the subject. I couldn't bring myself to speak about it further.

In retrospect, however, certain things he said stick with me.

A friend of mine, Phil, once asked Dad why so many bad things keep happening. Phil respected my father a great deal, as did many of my childhood friends. Dad coached several ball teams and didn't seem to mind that half the neighborhood played in our yard.

Phil's question to Dad had followed a game he'd pitched. Phil was complaining about close calls that went the wrong way, all of the school work he had to do, in addition to playing sports—the usual high school angst material.

At Phil's question, a slight smile crossed Dad's face. Somehow, he sensed there were larger implications. He placed his hand on Phil's shoulder and said, "I think God's a pretty smart guy. He probably knows what he's doing. You'll be fine."

Phil laughed good-naturedly, grasping that Dad understood his question all-too-well.

Without telling me, I think my father taught me how to handle tragedy better than any book, ethics course or preacher could have. Call it Faith of Our Fathers, if you will.

I observe the senseless, crueler side of nature on a regular basis. Working with trees and spending as much time in the wilderness as I do, I am privileged to witness the beauty of this planet and see a grandeur about nature that often leaves me speechless. But, to stick my head in the sand and deny nature's cavalier attitude would be, and certainly in my profession, down-right dangerous.

I don't know how Dad overcame his unimaginable loss. But somehow, he did. In doing so, he made it possible to eventually marry my mother and, fortunate for me and my brother and two sisters, have four more children.

Trees grow and trees will fall. Dad taught me how to live without a shadow in my soul. He showed me that I don't need to be constantly looking over my shoulder. He showed me how to embrace sunrises without reminding myself, the sun also sets.

DARK PINE

"There are no uninteresting things, only uninterested people."

~G.K. Chesterton

MY FAVORITE TREE IS A MASSIVE, WEATHER-BEATEN PINE THAT STANDS ALONE ATOP A remote outer island off the north shore of Isle Royale. The pine is so weathered, so windswept and rugged, so statuesque, that I think the tree deserves an island all to itself in the midst of the largest lake in the world. The name of the island where the pine lives is Dead Horse Rocks.

It is reported that Dead Horse Rocks was named by Wayne "Mack" McPherren, a fisherman who resided on Isle Royale in the late 1800s. It's reported that he chose the peculiar name because when he approached the island from his cabin on Captain Kidd Island—not exactly a normal north country name either—he thought the pine's island looked like a dead horse lying semi-submerged in the water. I've seen dead moose washed ashore in nearby Lane Cove, but never a dead horse. The islands don't resemble anything close to what I imagine a floating dead horse to look like.

Dead Horse Rocks actually consist of three long slender islands. They line up end-to-end and are so close together they almost touch. Combined, they stretch 1,000 feet long. But, they are only 70 feet wide at their widest point. The two smaller western-most islands barely break the surface of the water. The eastern-most island is the largest of the three, and has a 40-foot high rocky hump that runs down the length of it. There is a depression near the midway point that forms a natural hollow. In the hollow grows my favorite tree.

Due to exposure to the brunt of what Lake Superior can throw at it, the islands are primarily covered with wind-battered, ground-hugging plants such as lichen, moss, carpet juniper, blueberry and periwinkle. There are a few short scrawny trees that also live there—mountain ash, cedar, spruces and other pines.

None are more than 20-feet tall. The trees grow less than an inch per year due to Superior's icy gales. The stunted vegetation reminds me more of a tundra habitat than of the normal boreal forests of the Upper Great Lakes.

These outer islands are the only place where I've seen seagulls land in trees. The gulls are attracted to the berries from the mountain ash, but have a difficult time maintaining their balance on branches too small for their broad, webbed feet. Others attempt to hover beside the trees to pick off the berries. Seagulls are no hummingbirds. They can hover for only a second or two.

My pine is not tall as white pines go. It's only about 70-feet tall. But growing atop the island's ridge adds another thirty feet to it when you look at it from the water in a canoe. The pine towers over the other plants and small trees. The pine stands out so prominently that I've often seen eagles use its limbs as a lookout perch.

The storms take running starts at the pine. Winds race down from Canada, gaining momentum over the lake and land haymakers on its crown. It's like the old boy stepped forward from the forests of Isle Royale's main island and said to Goliath, "Take your best shot." And, like the old warrior he is, the tree has lost some battles. The top has been snapped off several times. Pines grow two new leads when they lose their main lead—the place where you would set the tree-top ornament. As a result, the pine has grown four dominant leads. One of which is missing, evident by the jagged stub that remains. Visible lightning scars run up and down the trunk, and it's anyone's guess as to how many times the tree's been struck. Lightning does not always leave streaks or wounds.

One year, I brought a measuring tape to determine the trunk's girth, which is 57 inches in diameter. The trunk has dark, blackish-gray bark that's at least four inches thick and appears so tough it would deflect bullets. The bark is covered with crusty lichen and stiff, brittle mosses that cause the tree to look so ancient you wonder if it's been there since the dawn of time. Where the trunk meets the ground, the buttress roots swell, separate and sprawl. Smaller woody roots spider across the top of the shallow, gravelly soil and it's not clear whether the tree is clutching the ground or the roots have transformed into living stone.

I've asked several island people about the tree—park rangers, fishermen, regular park visitors—and they all scratch their heads and say they don't recall such a tree. Even the research scientists, people who ought to notice, struggle to picture it. The thought that this David and Goliath death match, that this lightning-scarred warrior draws so little attention is puzzling. The lack of attention makes me feel all the more close to it. I have friends who claim they prefer the company of their dog or cat to that of other people. To them, I say, "I know what you mean."

The pine on Dead Horse Rocks is a remarkable tree, and, of all the trees I have seen, professionally or otherwise, it is the single toughest tree I've ever known. One day, it will inevitably fall to a Lake Superior gale. When the time comes, he will return his last bits of nourishment borrowed from Dead Horse Rocks. For a tree is married to the land it dwells on, and more faithful partners cannot be found.

I have a history with old pines.

When we vacationed at my grandparents' cottage near Grayling, Michigan, Dad would take my sisters and brother and me to Hartwick Pines State Park, located just north of Grayling. Major Edward E. Hartwick, for whom the park is named, made his fortune toward the end of the 19th century in various enterprises, including real estate, logging, mining and marketing his military fame. He rode with Teddy Roosevelt's Rough Riders during the Spanish-American War, and helped lead the famous charge up San Juan Hill. Major Hartwick died overseas during World War I. After he passed away, his wife, Karen Michelson Hartwick, purchased over 8,000 acres of land from the Salling-Hanson Company, a timber concern. The land, at the time, included 85 acres of never-been-cut old growth pine.

Mrs. Hartwick then donated the land to the State of Michigan with the stipulation that it serve as a memorial park for her late husband. To commemorate the logging history in the Grayling area, she requested a museum be built. In 1934 and 1935, a Civilian Conservation Corps work crew built two log structures to tell the tale of the "shanty boys," the men who turned Michigan's vast forests into the saw-timber that built the Midwest.

When I was a child, the main attraction at Hartwick Pines was the "Monarch Pine." Standing 181 feet tall, with a trunk diameter of 62 inches, and a lifespan of almost 400 years, it was an impressive sight. For decades, the Monarch Pine was the biggest tree in the preserve, possibly in the state. In those days, you could walk right up and touch it. The park service encouraged it, in fact. I remember placing my back to the trunk, tipping my head skyward to peer at branches that seemed to dwell in the clouds. Despite its massive size, the tree swayed in the wind ... sort of. The tree was so large that the sways didn't synchronize with the gusts, but would behave similar to turning a large ship. When you turn the wheel, the ship is so massive it doesn't begin its turn for several seconds.

I can recall the sound of Monarch Pine swaying in the wind. The sound had a distinctive note—a deep, solid-sounding wooden groan. As if heavy timbers are asked to bear too much weight. Young trees will squeak in high winds. Their branches rattle. But the deep resonating groan of a swaying Monarch is altogether different. It makes you want to back away from it. It made me feel as if the distant overhead needles were whispering messages I wasn't meant to hear.

On the drive to Hartwick Pines, Dad would tell us he wanted us kids to see virgin timber, and experience what the state looked like before it was all logged-off. Dad was an engineer by trade and had a passion for the hard sciences, especially physics. Neither Dad, nor Grandpa who was in advertising, ever talked much about the life-sciences, not even forestry, despite our last name. (Perhaps some long dormant gene sprang to the forefront in me.)

In hindsight, I believe my Mom and Dad were also looking for an excuse to escape the cramped quarters of my grandparents' cottage where we spent our summer vacations. Hartwick Pines was only 30 miles away. When rainy weather drove my cousins and siblings inside, it didn't take long to fray the adults' nerves. And despite the opportunity offered my grandparents to enjoy a few brief hours of peace, they always came along. Grandma would say, "We'll get more than enough quiet when you all go home next week." Grandpa was always eager to go. He, too, must have had some latent forester gene, as he was constantly planting trees at the cottage, despite its wooded surroundings. Though, he planted them too close to each other. He would always tell us he'd thin them out later. Yet he never did.

During our visits to Hartwick Pines, Grandpa would talk about Michigan's logging history. Born in 1894, my grandfather had witnessed the fall of the last giants. His father owned an ice business outside of Lansing, Michigan. The ice was cut from lakes and hauled by teams of horses to straw-filled barns, where the blocks would be stored. My grandfather inherited a few old photographs of his dad's business. There are no trees in the pictures. I've noticed the same lack of trees in other photographs from that era. Not long after the turn of the 20th century, Michigan became one big tract of stumps. He had witnessed all of that—the siltation of the trout streams, the elimination of game fish from Lakes Michigan, Huron and Erie, and the extinction of the Grayling. He'd seen slash-fires, where leftover treetops dried to tinder and when sparked, exploded into flame. He said when conditions dampened enough to allow people to safely burn, the smell of wood-smoke hung in the air for days, sometimes weeks.

My grandparents bought their cottage in 1957, well after virgin timber graced the property. By then, the land had filled in with young aspen and birch and maple—early succession trees. Aspen and birch are species that prefer full sun and often are the first to emerge after a clear-cut or fire.

He sold the cottage in the early 1970s while I was attending college at Michigan Tech. I was crushed by the news. My grandparents were getting up in age and likely needed the money from the sale. There were few pensions available to people of his generation. Having absolutely no money myself—and in hock to Dad for tuition—I still considered trying to buy the cottage. I'd loved its isolated lakeside setting in the woods.

After the sale, I didn't return to Hartwick Pines for 20 years.

We were heading north on I-75 to visit my wife's family in the Upper Peninsula, a ten-hour drive from Grand Rapids. On the way, I mentioned the Monarch Pine to her. "We ought to take our kids to see Hartwick Pines," I said.

"You know—let them see some real trees. It would help break up the long drive."
She agreed. When we stopped, I was happy to see the park hadn't changed much.
But when we walked down the path to view the Monarch Pine, I gasped, "Oh
no!" The tree was in terrible condition, and clearly dying. The top 20 feet was
already dead, and the remaining lower limbs were stunted, the needles yellowing.

At the potential loss of this State treasure, I felt shocked. Why isn't this
tree being cared for? Why aren't the dead limbs pruned-off? Why isn't someone
feeding it? Circling the tree, scrutinizing its condition, oblivious to the stares of
other park visitors, I couldn't help but say aloud, "This is a crime!"

We found the park headquarters and I approached the ranger who looked
to be in charge. I explained that I was an arborist and asked rather pointedly,
"What's being done to save Monarch Pine?"

He gave me a *"What are you talking about"* look and said, "Hartwick
Pines State Park is a forest preserve, sir. Here we allow nature to take its course.
No human intervention is allowed unless required for visitors' safety."

Not sensing that he saw any contradiction in calling the park a preserve,
yet not preserving the Monarch Pine, I argued, "This is a landmark tree, a tree
that can't be replaced. You are supposed to save trees like this. That's what
preservation means. Don't you think that requires more than doing nothing?"

The ranger crossed his arms at his chest, his back rigid, a posture rangers
do so well, and replied in an official tone. "Thank you for your suggestion,
sir. We appreciate your concern. You may write a letter to the superintendent if
you'd like."

Turning to another visitor at the counter, the ranger asked if he could help
them. Our conversation, apparently, was over.

If it weren't for the two Park Services—State and National—I would
never have known either of "my" pine trees. And, if it wasn't for their dogged
adherence to park policies, both of the Dead Horse Rocks and Monarch Pines
would have been cut down long ago. So I am grateful for all of their hard work
and efforts. But their rigid adherence to a hands-off policy doomed the biggest
and best tree in the state to an early demise.

The Monarch Pine died a few years later, in 1996. There were only a
couple of green branches left to the tree. The Park Service was forced to remove
the tree to protect visitors from its inevitable fall. The news of its felling was
reported in newspapers across the state.

*

There are several famous trees in the U.S. They too receive recognition.
I have visited The Monterey Pine in Monterey, California, which is said to be
the most photographed tree in the world. It grows in a similar situation to the
pine on Dead Horse Rocks. The Monterey Pine stands alone atop a pinnacle of

stone along the Pacific Ocean. It is located a couple of miles south of Pebble Beach where the U.S. Open is played. Road signs point the way to the tree. To ensure the Monterrey Pine remains upright, it's reinforced with guy-wires. It is regularly pruned, and is constantly tended to. Security cameras monitor the site around the clock.

The Methuselah Bristlecone Pine is located in the White Mountains in Inyo County in eastern California. It, too, is monitored, but its exact location is withheld from the public. The pine is estimated to be around 4,800 years old, and believed to be the world's oldest, non-clonal living plant.

The General Sherman Sequoia in Sequoia National Park, estimated to weigh 2.7 million pounds, is reputed to be the largest single plant by volume. (I fall on the side of those who don't believe a spreading subsurface fungus, or the rhizome-linked root system of an aspen grove count as a single plant.) The General Sherman is also monitored and nurtured.

The Joshua trees in Joshua Tree National Park, located northeast of Palm Springs, California, are similar to bristlecone pines in their longevity. Many of the trees are over a thousand years old. Two other attributes make them unique. They thrive in the desert and botanically speaking they're not a tree, but a succulent. Joshua trees stand upright, their limbs stretched out, thus earning them honorary tree status.

My pine on Dead Horse Rocks has received no recognition, let alone care. But there is at least one heralded tree on Lake Superior. The Minnesota Hat Point Cedar has been mentioned in Jesuit journals dating back to the mid-1600s. The Hat Point Cedar was used as a landmark by Native Americans and voyageurs paddling the north shore of Lake Superior. The tree helped them to locate nearby portage routes. Many Native Americans to this day attribute spiritual qualities to the Hat Point Cedar.

There are other trees that receive special recognition, and not for their size or age. Trees are often planted as living memorials for loved ones who've passed away. Upon request, the local university, Grand Valley State University, plants trees with red foliage to commemorate students who've died while attending school. Few people know about the memorial trees. The university does not allow plaques nor advertise their designation. It's sobering to see how many dark, burgundy-leafed trees there are scattered across campus. I can understand why the school doesn't make the information common knowledge. I am sometimes asked to maintain memorial trees by the parents of lost children. It is some of my most gratifying and anxiety-ridden work that I do. It's one of those, "Please don't perish on my watch" responsibilities.

No other plant reminds us more of ourselves than trees do. They are long-lived. They stand upright. They have limbs and twiggy fingers and a vascular system. They grace our homes. They lend an aesthetic quality to our lives that's palpable. Their environmental benefits are immeasurable.

*

It is a twenty minute paddle from the campground at Belle Isle to my pine on Dead Horse Rocks. The north shore of Isle Royale is generally considered the more remote part of the Park. Approaching the rocks, I feel the pine's presence. It's a feeling I'm not comfortable admitting to. It seems inappropriate, as if I'm losing objectivity, losing my grasp of science. To be clear, I'm not saying I feel an aura emanate from the tree or sense weird vibrations. It's nothing I can really place a finger on. I don't normally look to trees for anything more than metaphorical guidance. I've made it a practice not to hug trees, and it may sound like I'm contradicting myself, I think it unwise to grow too cozy with them. They certainly don't cozy up to me. I've been hit on the head more than once by falling limbs when pruning. With that said, I can't help but walk up and touch the tree I'm inspecting.

The biggest reason I was bothered by nobody trying to save Monarch Pine, besides fear for its loss, is that it's so contrary to the mission. Wilderness preservation and its close counterpart, tree preservation, have always meant more than merely keeping the humans away. The creation of Isle Royale National Park as a wilderness area is a perfect example. It has taken over 80 years and tens of millions of dollars to restore an island that by the early twentieth century had its rock blasted for copper, a third of its forests cleared, the small game trapped-out, and the big-game completely hunted out.

Fortunately for us, with the onset of the Great Depression, the mining and timber companies who owned over 90 percent of Isle Royale were eager to sell their lands to the Park Service. During those hard times, many of the resort and summer cottage owners also quickly agreed to terms, though some residents still resist. I doubt that if the business concerns had been thriving the movement to turn the island into a national park would have gained traction. The island almost certainly would have evolved into valuable lakefront property, its shoreline fringed with high-end summer homes. "No Trespass" signs would be tacked to several of the trees.

In 1926, Albert Stoll, a reporter for the *Detroit News*, took a three-day boat trip from Detroit to Isle Royale. He spent the next two weeks as a resort guest. He became so enamored with the place that when he returned to the newspaper, he wrote a series of articles promoting Isle Royale as a state park. When the State turned the idea down, his editor suggested he promote the island as a national park. Several other Michigan newspapers soon picked up the cause.

An official request was eventually made to James Mather, the National Park Superintendent, to visit Isle Royale and see for himself why the island qualified. After his visit, Mr. Mather was quoted as saying, "The Island exemplifies everything a National Park should be." In 1931, Congress declared

Isle Royale the second National Park to be established east of the Mississippi, Arcadia National Park in Maine being the first. Yet, due to the hard times of the 1930s, the park's dedication service wasn't held until 1941.

Over the years, the Park Service has demolished all but two of the island's old resorts. They have removed the golf course at Belle Isle and most of the fish camps that once dotted the island. They have burned the slash that loggers left behind. Ranger stations, fire towers and docks have been built and trail crews have created over 200 miles of hiking trails connecting 30 campgrounds. Beyond that, the island has been left natural, returning Isle Royale over the past 80 years into a wilderness park that many consider the "Jewel of the National Park Service."

Many of the Isle Royale rangers I've talked to have worked at other National Parks, most famously in the West. When asked which park is their favorite, almost every ranger hedges a bit, embarrassed, as if they've been asked to pick their favorite child. What they will admit to is, "Isle Royale is the one park that best exemplifies wilderness."

Isle Royale is a tremendous success story. Hartwick Pines, in contrast, is more of a historical monument. That's not a criticism, just a more accurate description. A hundred years after its dedication, only 40 acres of virgin pines remain at Hartwick Pines, and there's no hope of saving those trees for future generations. They're fading. Trees do not live forever—even with the best of care. The pines are succumbing to forest succession. With some care, if any is allowed, the virgin trees might last a hundred more years. But when the last pine falls, no vestige will remain of Michigan's primordial forests.

Wilderness preservation is a hands-on project. It involves far more than stopping development. Preservation is taking proactive measures to restore native habitats: eliminate invasive species (be they plant or animal), repair stream banks, remove unnecessary structures, replant appropriate trees, understory plants, grasses and groundcover. Wilderness preservation means building hiking trails that navigate visitors away from nesting sites. It's restoring native fish by not only restricting catches and policing fishermen, but by restocking. And lest it's forgotten, creating or restoring a wilderness, saving an old-growth forest, and rescuing an endangered species requires lots of money. I think it would have been okay to spend a little on caring for the Monarch Pine.

The Monarch Pine and the pine on Dead Horse Rocks represent more than the last hold-outs of a "treed" nation, whose brothers fell to a misguided notion of Manifest Destiny. Preserving them also represents an admission of error, an attempt to correct a great wrong. They represent contrition. Seen in a more positive light, they also represent what can be achieved.

At one time, foresters only managed forests to produce a cash crop. But in this era, many foresters also work for more altruistic reasons: to promote recreational use, produce wildlife habitat or nurture endangered species. They manage forests to prevent hillsides from eroding into streams and rivers and lakes. Forests are managed for research purposes. Amazingly, there are now pockets of woodlands where foresters intentionally allow trees to simply grow old, to become old growth forests, once again.

Arborists also do the same. We just do it one tree at a time.

When the time comes, I was going to ask my sons to spread my ashes at the feet of the pine on Dead Horse Rocks. Both of our sons have been there. The first time that Nick, our youngest, saw the pine, an eagle sat on an upper limb. The eagles do not nest in the tree, but this particular eagle gave Nick and I the distinct impression the pine belonged to him, not to us. The feeling was so pronounced that we waited in the canoe well-offshore until after he flew away. Only then did we step ashore.

I had also never mentioned my wishes for my final destination to Ken, my best friend and long-time Isle Royale canoe partner. Almost every September for over 30 years Ken and I have spent a week in the Park, camping and fishing. The year that Ken's father passed away, three weeks before leaving for our island trip, I found out from his sister that Ken planned to spread his dad's ashes at Dead Horse Rocks, in the shallows beneath the pine. I swallowed hard and said nothing.

Despite needing to deal with his Dad's estate, and with our trip only three weeks after the funeral, Ken's daughters still encouraged him to go to Isle Royale with me. They thought it a needed vacation following what had been a long bedside vigil and months of care-giving. His daughters also thought the island ceremony an appropriate way to honor their grandfather's life. Ken's dad was an avid outdoorsman.

When we arrived on Isle Royale, Ken constructed a three-foot tall cross from driftwood we found on a nearby beach. He lashed the two cross members together with vines and some twine we brought with us. We then had to wait three days for the winds to calm enough for us to canoe out to Dead Horse Rocks.

At dawn, on a beautiful, crystal-aired, Lake Superior day, Ken and I loaded up the canoe, shoved off, and paddled out to the pine. As Dead Horse Rocks is due east of the campground, we watched the sun crest the Greenstone Ridge over the prow of the canoe. The pine glowed in the morning light and grew larger as we approached.

We set ashore onto a small gravel beach scooped out of the rocks right beneath the tree. Ken removed from his pack the urn and a couple of other items he'd brought for the ceremony. I lifted the cross out of the canoe. Together, we piled fist-size rocks around the base of the cross to support it against a boulder at the top of the beach, well above high-water line. Once secure, we picked berries, sprigs of periwinkle and cedar, and draped them on the cross member and around the foot of the cross. We cut evergreen boughs and spread them about the site and scattered more mountain ash berries and wild rose blossoms atop the boughs.

When we finished, Ken waded into the lake, gently spread his father's ashes into Lake Superior and said, "Here you go Dad."

The marker stands there today. We return each year to repair any damages and to add fresh greens and flowers.

A better way to commemorate a father's life, I cannot imagine.

Nobody seems to notice the marker. Like the tree itself. Perhaps, it draws no notice because the grayed driftwood blends so well into the stone-colored lichen growing on the boulder. It could simply be because the site is so remote that nobody visits. It could also be that, out of respect, people don't mention it.

I don't know what possessed Ken to do the following but when he did, I felt he'd done more justice to the pine than anything I would have thought to request.

On the north side of the tree, the side that can't be seen from the water, Ken placed a poem to honor his father. He'd laminated the poem before leaving for the island to protect the sheet of paper from the weather. He then framed it with slender pine branches, cut to fit.

After tacking the framed poem to the tree, we bowed our heads, said some prayers and then Ken said a few words about his Dad's life and influence.

They were respectful words…words filled with his love for his father. When he finished the eulogy, he asked if I would read the poem aloud since he didn't think he could.

DARK PINE
by Robert Service

If my life-force, by death decree,
Could find green haven in a tree,
And there in peace untroubled years
Could dream, immune from toil and tears,
Though I'm a lover of all trees
I would not favour one of these...

I would not choose a brittle palm
Beside a sea of senile calm;
Or willow droopily adream
Above bright babble of a stream.
No cypress would inhibit me
With dark and dour austerity;
Nor olive, shattering the light,
Nor poplar, purple in the night.
The sanctuary of my search
Would not be oak, nor ash, nor birch:
Ah no! Their comfort I decline, -
Let my life-force pervade a Pine.

Aye, when my soul shall say forth
Let it be to the naked North,
And in a lone pine desolate
Achieve its fit and final fate;
A pine by arctic tempest torn,
Snow scourged, wind savaged and forlorn;
A Viking trunk, a warrior tree,
A hostage to dark destiny
Of iron earth and icy sky,
That valiantly disdains to die.

This is the home where I would bide,
If trees like men had souls inside, -
Which is, of course, a fantasy
None could conceive but dolts like me...
Let others vision Heaven's gate,
Dark Pine, I dream for me you wait.

THE GREEN MENACE

*"The larger the island of knowledge,
the longer the shoreline of wonder."*

~Ralph W. Sockman

THE STAY AT BELLE ISLE CAMPGROUND HAD BEEN IDEAL. FISHING WAS OUTSTANDING, the weather perfect. I visited Dead Horse Rocks almost daily. I ended up staying 10 days at Belle Isle instead of the planned seven. I'd stayed so long that I'd settled into a routine, which was something I'd hoped to avoid. I could sense I was becoming too sedentary, too comfortable, too ruled by habit. Life back home was ruled by habits—habits that may ensure I accomplish essential tasks, but they also cause me to go on autopilot. I certainly didn't want to go through the motions here. As much as I hated to leave Belle Isle, I needed to go.

When planning the itinerary for a month at Isle Royale, I decided to do a slow circle of the eastern half of the park. On my dining room table at home on a yellow legal pad, I broke the month into four week-long segments. The actual length of stay at each camp would depend on the weather and on fishing. Fish formed the mainstay of dinners. And from past trips to Isle Royale (I'd been going for twenty years by this time), I'd grown to prefer establishing base camps as opposed to travelling every day. Staying in one place allows enough time to not only locate fish, but to more thoroughly explore the surrounding area.

I selected the four base camps largely due to their isolation and difficulty to reach. It's not that I'm anti-social, but when I go to Isle Royale I'm not there to make friends. Most people seek out wilderness areas, as I do, to enjoy a human-free environment. For me that rules out big camping parties. Over the years, many friends and family have hinted at wanting to come along. The island has been the one place I don't invite them to. I've never gone to Isle Royale with anyone besides Ken or my sons.

The first week was to be spent at Belle Isle, my favorite campground. It is located on an outer island off the more remote north shore. Hikers can't reach Belle Isle unless they take the water taxi, which is a pricey way to travel for typically economy-minded backpackers, and once there, there are no trails. Kayakers frequent Belle Isle, but in reduced numbers since they must paddle completely around the island to get there and travel past treacherous Blake Point. The point can be a dicey venture. It is fully exposed and currents converge to form steep, disjointed waves.

I planned to spend the second week at McCargo Cove. It's a quiet campsite, even by Isle Royale standards. It is accessible to backpackers, but is a good two-day hike from Rock Harbor, where most visitors disembark. That eliminates many people. The average length of stay on the island is four days. A two day hike to McCargo Cove and a two day hike back doesn't allow anytime for exploring the island on a four-day trip.

For the third week, I'd return to the south shore through a chain of inland lakes and set up camp at Chippewa Harbor. It's only six miles across the island from McCargo Cove to Chippewa Harbor, but the trails between the lakes must be crossed three times since it takes two trips to shuttle the canoe and the packs between lakes. The trek also entails going over the Greenstone Ridge again. It would be a tough day, but worth it, or so I thought when planning the trip. The campground is set inside a short channel connecting Chippewa Lake to Lake Superior and is one of the most picturesque locations on the island.

The West Caribou Island Campground, which is tucked just inside the western entry to Rock Harbor, would be my fourth and final base camp. Rock Harbor is nine miles long and is the longest stretch of protected water on the island. At the northeast end of Rock Harbor are the ferry dock, ranger station, lodge and hospitality cabins. At the opposite end of the harbor is Moskey Basin and its crescent-shaped beach. Camp shelters ring the beach and offer a view down the entire length of Rock Harbor, and I almost selected Moskey Basin for the last camp site, but the basin is beside one of the most frequently used trails on Isle Royale and the fishing can be iffy.

All four of the campgrounds I chose offer Adirondack-style shelters. The shelters provide a roof over your head, plenty of room to spread out your gear and a raised floor that gets you off the ground. The extra room and roof have obvious benefits. But the raised floor may be the greatest. It often rains on Isle Royale. Dews are heavy in the morning. The ground is typically damp until 10 a.m. Keeping clothes and bedrolls dry is critical to being comfortable. I packed a tent in case the shelters were full, but thankfully, never needed it.

I would not spend the entire month alone. My oldest son, Sam, was joining me for the first five days. He had just turned 25, and I would turn 50 while staying on the island – two momentous birthdays. I was thrilled that he could come along, and he was a huge help hauling everything over the Greenstone Ridge to reach Belle Isle that first day.

Ken would join me for the fourth and final week. Both Sam and Ken brought enough food for those two weeks we'd spend together. That meant I only had to pack enough food for the two middle weeks of my stay, which helps explain, in part, how I managed to carry a month's worth of supplies on my back. It was a question I was often asked by other campers who rarely stay for more than a week and whose packs always seem stuffed to the brim. The other explanation is meal planning.

Breakfasts consisted of instant oatmeal or pancakes, the just-add-water varieties. The powders are light and easily pack into baggies that form-fit inside backpacks. I also took pre-cooked bacon that only needs to be heated to prepare.

For lunches, I ate a couple of sticks of elk jerky that Ken had provided for my trip. I also eat a couple slices of cheese, and for dessert, a candy bar. Eating cold lunches is by design. I didn't want to stop in the middle of the day to build a fire or break out a stove. "We're burning daylight" is an apt expression for places where there's no electricity. In September, the days grow shorter and daylight is indeed precious. Cold lunches also reduce the amount of stove fuel I carry, which lightens the load. Liquids are by nature, heavy.

For dinners, I ate lake trout or salmon when fishing Lake Superior. When fishing the inland lakes I dined on walleye or pike. Fortunately, I caught fish nearly every day and never tired of it. There were a few long days spent on the water. But for fishermen that is not considered work, and I cannot overemphasize how important or how delicious fresh fish tastes. Not to brag, but those meals were as grand as any 5-star restaurant's rendition.

When I felt the need for an energy burst, I would eat raisins or candy bars, as I'm allergic to nuts. I do tend to go a little overboard on packing Milky Ways and Kit Kat bars, and has anyone else besides Ken and I noticed how attractive the Sun Maid raisin girl is on the front of the box? After dinner, I ate popcorn. The aroma of hot buttered popcorn mixed with the cool scent of conifers is a delicious smell, though a confusing one. It brings thoughts of dark movie theaters transported into the pinewoods.

If I say so myself, all the planning paid off. I was warm and dry every night, and I never went hungry.

Still, after ten days at Belle Isle, I needed to move on. Canoeing alone, the paddle from Belle Isle to McCargo Cove takes six-to-eight hours, and most of it is on protected waters — through Robinson Bay and Pickerel Cove or through the Amygdaloid Channel depending on which route you choose. The paddle still requires light winds so as to safely negotiate a three-mile open-water portion that can't be avoided. The open waters of Lake Superior are not a place to dally in a canoe. I can testify that plying waves greater than two-feet is pushing your luck. Winds can change direction and change intensity as if the weather gods flicked a switch. I always breathe easier once I pass between the buoys at the mouth of McCargo Cove.

The cove is a spectacular place to paddle a canoe. By Great Lakes standards, McCargo Cove is as close to a fjord as they come. Steep, forested hillsides border both sides of the deep, narrow, two-mile inlet. The cove is also the only body of water that cuts against the grain of the parallel ridges that run the length of Isle Royale. McCargo Cove has other unique traits. If you're more than a mile off shore, the entry is invisible. It's as if the island is trying to hide its soft-spot. A natural outcrop extends across the cove's mouth, causing the entry to make a 90 degree turn where it empties into Lake Superior. The outcrop serves as a natural breakwall, and from a mile out, the camouflage of rock and trees screens the entry so effectively that British Captain Robert McCargo, for whom the cove is named, used it to hide his schooner, The Recovery, during the War of 1812. His sailors are reported to have lowered their sails and disassembled the masts so passing American frigates wouldn't spot the ship protruding above the treetops. The entry hasn't changed much from those days. The buoys that mark the channel are small and subtle, barely four feet high, and painted drab red and green.

Throughout the last half of the 19th century, a mining camp of some 200 men existed at the far end of the cove, where the campground is now located. The community was busy, though not too thriving. Despite the more than half-million tons of copper shipped out of McCargo Cove, the costs to operate the nearby mine made all three attempts to procure copper unprofitable. Today, no trace of the old waterside town remains. Without the historical plaque posted near the dock, you wouldn't recognize the site as being anything other than a secluded wilderness campground.

Sound reverberates up and down the length of the cove. The slam of a shelter door or the clang of pots will echo. Raised voices do the same. As a result, campers tend to talk in hushed tones. Canada geese, several species of ducks and the common loon grace the smooth waters. Loons can be heard day and night. Their trills add emphasis to the quiet North Country setting. Gliding into McCargo Cove in a canoe at the end of a day of fishing, with loon-song filling the air, is the way I'd like to drive home from work every day.

This year, a new sign is posted at the dock, and it has nothing to do with island history. It is a warning to thoroughly clean all fishing gear, paddles, canoes and kayaks before venturing into the interior.

I'd already been warned about the new requirement by Carl TerHaar, the park ranger who patrols the north shore. Carl appeared to me to be a man of few words, but I had seen him almost daily at the Belle Isle Campground. During one of our brief conversations, he told me he'd worked on the island for nearly 30 years and, in a rare self-revealing moment, said he was retiring soon. I was sorry to hear it.

Carl also informed me that the stream from Chickenbone Lake to McCargo Cove was closed to paddlers to prevent contamination. The news was disappointing. I had planned to use the stream. Its slow-moving water allows an extra quarter-mile float versus portaging. When carrying heavy canoes and packs, floating an extra quarter mile is appreciated.

The reason the Park Service closed the stream, he told me, was to avoid introducing invasive species to the inland waters. Carl shrugged when he told me about the closing. He gave me the impression that he felt it wouldn't make any appreciable difference in stopping exotic species since countless waterfowl wing between Lake Superior and the inland lakes. Any number of them could easily transport spiny water fleas or excrete zebra mussel eggs into streams and lakes.

Carl said, "I suppose it can't hurt to be on the safe side. Just be sure to clean off the bottom of your canoe and watch out for any hitchhikers on hooks and leaders."

The stream closing irked me, and my degree of annoyance felt greater than it should be. I was angrier than what an extra portage distance should cause or the extra chores. It's not a big chore to clean the canoe and tackle, and it was certainly good advice. The Park Service had every reason to initiate the new precaution. Nonetheless, the closing rankled me, and my strong reaction made me stop to examine why I felt so angry.

Then the light bulb went on. It wasn't the extra work that irked me. It was the reminder of work.

Recently, at the tree service, we weren't just neck deep in invasive pest control, we were over our heads in it. Japanese beetles, hemlock wooly adelgids, Asian Long Horned Beetles, gypsy moths—and my most recent nemesis, the emerald ash borer—all served up a broad palette of invasive pest work. And those were just the insects. We had also begun to work for the State of Michigan in its fight against invasive plants and diseases. The list is long. Autumn olive, buckthorn, purple loosestrife, spotted spurge, black locust, phragmites, honeysuckle, sweet clover, Oriental bittersweet, Japanese knotweed, Oak Wilt, beech bark disease, Dutch elm disease—even the once landscape favorite, Norway maple—were all on the State's hit-list.

The issue with invasive species is they wreak havoc to natural pest and prey balances. Fortunately for Isle Royale, Lake Superior forms a formidable barrier for them. But, if given a toe-hold, the spread of exotic pests would be almost impossible to stop. Once established, eradication would entail physical removal, pesticides or control-burns—none of which are gentle remedies. In fact, the remedies can, at times, causes more damage than the problem they are trying to resolve.

Invasive species may be the biggest biological threat to the Great Lakes Region, if not to the planet as a whole. And I knew that all-to-well. And for four wonderful weeks I didn't want to think about invasive pests, and especially didn't want to think about what damage they might inflict to Isle Royale.

Isle Royale National Park is the very definition of a Great Lakes wilderness, so much so, that the United Nations declared the park an International Biosphere Preserve. The island hosts several scientific studies, and has become, in essence, the control subject to a great experiment. It is the place where researchers go to witness firsthand how a purely native habitat behaves. It is an example that is becoming increasingly rare.

No. I didn't want to think about invasive species and particularly didn't want to be reminded of the damn emerald ash borer ... the ash killer ... the tree terminator.

Most insects don't cause a tree to drop dead practically overnight. Native insects take several years to overwhelm a tree. Native pests are kept in check by their predators, such as parasitic wasps, ladybugs, woodpeckers, etc. Typically, it is only weaker trees that succumb to pests. They are the trees that suffer from storm or drought or flood damage or sudden changes to their habitat. Their defense mechanisms are weakened. Many botanists believe pests are actually drawn to these trees, as if they emit a scent only an insect detects.

The emerald ash borer, on the other hand, attacks all ash trees, healthy or otherwise. The borers have no native predators to speak of. One year, homeowners notice a little die-off at the top of their tree and a proliferation of suckers growing along the main limbs and trunk. The next year, their tree is dead. Ash comprise up to 10 percent of the forests of North America. It's estimated that more than 8 billion trees will be lost to the emerald ash borer. That's enough trees to cover the Province of Ontario and the five Great Lake states combined, lakes included.

These sorts of infestations normally occur where one would expect an invasion to occur—on the East or West Coasts. Emerald ash borer, instead, snuck into the heartland through the St. Lawrence Seaway and established a beachhead in the town of my birth: Detroit, Michigan. Comfortably nestled in crate-wood made from ash cut in China, the emerald ash borer was shipped on international freighters to the Motor City.

Disembarking from the freighters sometime in the 1990s, the beetles quickly flew to nearby ash trees. Ash prefers moist lowland areas. Southeast Michigan and the Windsor Peninsula of Canada are almost nothing but lowlands. Five to 10 years later—an educated guess since nobody knows exactly when the emerald ash borer first arrived—thousands of ash trees began to mysteriously die.

Local arborists identified the epidemic as a borer insect, but one they'd never seen before. Forestry experts at Michigan State University were contacted, and Dr. Dave Roberts was one of the first entomologists to inspect the Detroit trees. When he didn't recognize the beetle, he suspected we were in trouble.

Dr. Roberts captured a few beetles—not an easy task since they are quick and can fly—and then took them back to his lab. He couldn't find the beetle in his entomology books or on any of the insect identification web sites. He sent samples to colleagues, who couldn't identify them, either. Dr. Roberts eventually shipped the bugs to the National Entomological Library at the Smithsonian in Washington D.C. They also couldn't identify the insects. The Smithsonian eventually shipped them to the International Entomological Library in Greece, where they were finally identified by an Agrilus Specialist as (*Agrilus planipennis)*, the emerald ash borer.

Meanwhile, ash trees were continuing to die around southeast Michigan, and the situation was serious. When the American elm fell to Dutch elm disease in the 1940s and 1950s, many street trees were replanted with ash. By 2001, the ash trees were gaining enough size to recreate the arbor effect the elms had once provided. Ash made up 25 percent of all the street trees in the metro Detroit area. Millions more were planted in homeowners' yards. There were more than that growing wild in the surrounding woodlots and along the edge of lakes, streams and nearby Lake Erie and Lake St. Clair.

Part of the concern was that trees growing in urban areas are environmental workhorses. Centered where they can do the most good, urban trees reduce air pollutants and smog. They slow storm-water run-off. They cool streets and moderate heat-sinks. Urban trees convert excessive levels of CO_2 into oxygen and do so where it benefits the most people. City trees also provide a palpable green-relief for city dwellers.

But it wasn't the environmental or aesthetic loss that most concerned city and state officials.

It was the money.

The infestation couldn't have happened at a worse time. Already financially reeling from a major downturn of the auto industry, tax revenues for the City of Detroit and the State of Michigan had shrunk to where they barely covered essential services. Compared to staffing police and fire departments or maintaining streets and highways, saving trees fell way down the priority list.

The cost of removing all of the dead trees, let alone replacing them, would run into the hundreds of millions of dollars. And all of the dead trees standing alongside roadways were becoming increasingly brittle and dangerous. It became obvious to local and state authorities that this was a problem that had to be addressed. With tax revenues at their lowest levels since the Great Depression, the City of Detroit and the State of Michigan cried out for help. Perhaps no other tree better represents the gritty, proudly unpretentious, blue-collar people of Detroit. The ash is a barely noticed, ubiquitous tree. It has a forgettable green flower that more resembles a malformation than a blossom. Its autumn color is dull yellow or pale purple. The bark is non-descript and the branch structure is so normal it defies attention.

Plain, however, does not mean they're weak. Ash trees may be the perfect city tree. They are highly resistant to salt damage, which is a great attribute to have if you're planted above some of the largest salt mines in the world such as the mines under the City of Detroit, and whose streets are heavily salted during their long winters. Ash thrives in hard, compacted soils, which makes them ideal for parkways and parking lot islands. They barely notice floods or droughts. And, up until the emerald ash borer, they suffered from few pest problems. As a shade tree, ash quietly goes about its business of cooling and greening the neighborhoods they shelter.

Ash wood is tough. Baseball bats, hockey sticks, shovel and hammer handles are made from ash wood. It's used for lumber and trim work. Its grain is a clean, light vanilla color with few blemishes. Even the knots are hardly noticeable. And it has one other unique characteristic. Native Americans use ash trees for basket-making. Before the Europeans brought metal pots and cloth sacks to the "New World," Native Americans used animal skins and ash-baskets for food storage and to transport goods. Basket making was a highly respected craft—still is—and natives traveled for miles to trade with the better basket makers.

The Native Americans had discovered that the growth rings in ash trees are easily separated. By beating a freshly cut ash log with a heavy stick during early spring, the blows cause each year's growth rings to pop apart. Once separated, the quarter-inch thick wood can be scored length-wise and peeled into strips. There was a time when the thump of ash logs reverberated through the woods. Harvesting ash strips was as big a springtime activity as the more famous sugar bushing.

Fearful of the potential loss of ash trees, Sue, a fellow employee at the tree service and of Odawa descent, approached me with a letter from her elders. Sue participated in the local Pow Wows. She danced in traditional clothes that she'd hand-made for ceremonial events and is one of the most soft-spoken persons I know. The letter from the elders expressed the tribe's deep concerns about the fate of the ash tree. Sue asked if I would take the letter to the appropriate authorities to add her people's voices to the effort to stop the emerald ash borer.

McCargo Cove reminded me of Sue and of her elder's letter that I'd delivered. The outcrop that obscures the entry to the Cove is called Indian Point. It is easy to picture the camps that once stood there, the open-air fish-drying racks, the cooking fires. It's likely those Native Americans showed Captain McCargo where to hide his ship. The British, like the French before them, built trading posts inside the coves and bays up and down the shores of Lake Superior. A brisk trade lasted for two centuries. Furs were traded for manufactured goods. The Native Americans did most of the actual fur trapping.

McCargo Cove may have been named after a British skipper, but both ends of the portage route are named after the original trail blazers. Indian Point is the north end of the water trail, and across the island at the south end is Chippewa Harbor. Before the National Park Service maintained the portage route and before the miners and loggers used it for their cart path, the Ojibway, Odawa, Cree and other tribes of the Upper Great Lakes used the route to reach the siskiwit fishing grounds on the south side of Isle Royale. Native peoples ventured to Isle Royale from Canada, which is only 8 to 12 miles away. Archeological records show they'd been coming to Isle Royale for over 6,000 years. They would bisect the island via the portage route to reach the fishing grounds. In doing so, they were saving almost 50 miles of dangerous open-water canoeing to paddle around the island.

The siskiwit the Natives were after is a deepwater subspecies of lake trout. It normally inhabits waters 200 feet or deeper. But in the springtime, siskiwit, also known as "fat trout," migrate to the island's south side reefs to spawn in the bay named after them, Siskiwit Bay. Fat trout contain high concentrations of fish oil, which many think spoils the flavor. Having never eaten a Fat Trout, I couldn't say. But the Native peoples weren't after the fish for food. They wanted the siskiwit for their oil, which they used for medicinal purposes, ointments, and paints.

The Europeans and the Americans that followed them preferred whitefish for table fare. Tales of the delicious flavor of Lake Superior whitefish were recorded in journals of the earliest explorers. The annual spawning runs in the St. Mary's River, where Lake Superior flows into Lake Huron, brought indigenous people from all across the region to harvest the teeming whitefish. By all accounts, the annual run near current day Sault Ste. Marie was a major gathering of regional peoples. In addition to much trading, it was a time to exchange news, gossip and socialize. It's said that many spouses first met at these gatherings.

There are very few ash trees on Isle Royale, and I hadn't thought about the emerald ash borer since I arrived to the island. But Carl's instructions to sanitize my tackle, my paddling past Indian Point earlier in the day, and the new sign at the dock—all brought back to mind Sue's people's plea for help, as well as my own struggle to control the emerald ash borer for my client's trees.

About the time she gave me the letter, the State of Michigan had submitted their request for federal funding, knowing the money would have strings attached to it. The only way the Federal Government could become involved was if the State convinced them that the emerald ash borer would spread across state lines, which posed no problem to prove. They'd already spread into Ontario and were stepping on the doorstep of the City of Toledo, Ohio. What the State did find difficult to prove to the Feds was a way to completely eradicate the emerald ash borer. The latter stipulation meant Michigan needed to convince the Feds they could kill every last beetle. That's a tall order.

For a State to acquire funding from the Animal & Plant Health Inspection Service (APHIS), the federal agency that handles emergency infestations and epidemics, a panel of experts must write a grant proposal claiming what they hoped was a credible eradication strategy—a winning war plan. APHIS holds millions of dollars in reserve so it can adequately handle emergency epidemics or infestations that pose a serious threat to the health and/or livelihood of Americans. While the agency is more noted for dealing with salmonella outbreaks or hoof and mouth disease, they also cover tree infestations if given the right set of circumstances. To make their case, the State's panel of experts invited the Feds to Detroit to witness firsthand the outbreak.

The site they picked was a dentist office located within one of the rougher Detroit neighborhoods. Jane Oliver, who was one of the Michigan Department of Agriculture's inspector's, suggested the site. Her husband is the dentist who owned the office building. The property had several infested ash trees out front. On a pleasant Wednesday afternoon in June, twenty-one officials arrived at the property to examine the ash trees. The officials included Department of Agriculture inspectors, several U.S. and State foresters, the Michigan State University research team and, of course, the APHIS people from Washington. It was an impressive gathering of scientists and high-ranking local, state and federal officials. Dressed in professional attire—suits, ties, skirts or dress slacks—the group didn't exactly look like people from the neighborhood.

Unfortunately, a car full of gang members thought the same. They drove around the block once, then twice, and a couple more times to investigate further. A crowd of well-dressed, professionals milling around couldn't mean anything good for them. On their fourth lap, there were three loud pops followed by the sound of screeching tires.

Young, newly-hired Melinda Flores, wearing a pair of white cotton slacks that she'd bought for the meeting and the catered lunch to follow, slowly slumped to the ground, a crimson splotch slowly spreading across her thigh. She'd been standing at the back of the group closest to the street as Dr. Deborah McCullough peeled bark off a tree to reveal the larvae feeding in the cambium. Dr. McCullough reported later that she vaguely heard the pops and then heard this weak voice say, "I think I have a problem."

Turning to see what was wrong, the whole group was staring down at Melinda with puzzled looks, until somebody with more street smarts shouted, "Everybody down!"

Some hit the dirt, some simply stood there, not understanding, a couple of Melinda's associates rushed to her help. Cell phones sprang into action. Police arrived five minutes later and an ambulance shortly afterwards.

Thankfully, the bullet missed her femur and any major blood vessels.

The meeting was postponed. It took a couple of months for everyone to collect themselves. Once they did, the State panel re-invited the Washington officials back to Michigan, promising they'd pick a safer location. To their request, the Feds politely replied, "Why don't you come to Washington?"

In anticipation of receiving the federal funding, the Michigan Department of Agriculture (MDA) had hired and trained 100 people to determine the extent of the outbreak. The MDA called their new employees, "EAB Scouts." The scouts scattered across southeast Michigan and, within three months, located the leading edge of the infestation. They discovered that the insects inhabited a seven-county area. The Canadians were doing their own scouting and identified the extent of their outbreak in the Windsor Peninsula. Armed with the knowledge of the front lines, the MDA then assigned the panel of science experts to draft an eradication plan to procure the funding.

The eventual plan submitted to APHIS would leave many people—particularly us in the tree care business—stunned. Maybe it was the seriousness of the outbreak that caused the panel to overreach. Maybe it was because the panel consisted mostly of foresters, who when faced with big problems often revert to forest fire control tactics. Whatever the reasons, the eradication strategy they proposed was so colossal that nobody, at first, believed the communiqué they released was real.

To prove to APHIS they could eradicate the emerald ash borer and procure the desperately needed funding, the panel of experts proposed creating, in essence, a firebreak. They proposed removing every single ash tree in a 6-mile-wide, 500-mile-long ring around southeast Michigan. The Canadians proposed a similar 100-mile-long cutting that would stretch across the southern half of the Windsor Peninsula. The thinking was that by removing all of the ash trees just beyond the leading edge of the infestation zone, they would trap the insects inside. Similar to fighting a forest fire, once the ash borers met the ash-less firebreak, there'd be no more food to sustain them, since the emerald ash borer feeds only on ash trees. Trapped inside the ring, EAB could then be systematically eliminated via pesticides and/or tree removals. Either way, once enclosed, the beetles would eventually kill all of the ash trees inside the ring and then starve to death.

To an arborist, such as myself, the strategy had major flaws:

- The sheer size of the project. The proposed 6-mile wide, 500-mile long ring is 3,000 square miles in size and would entail removing millions of trees.
- The proposed cutting was almost completely on private property, much of it densely populated.
- Removing trees often requires heavy equipment.
- How would property owners be reimbursed for the damage caused to their property, not to mention reimbursed for the loss of trees?
- And most significantly was the belief, that the beetles could fly only six miles in any given year. It was why a six-mile-wide cutting was proposed. But what would happen if after removing the ring of trees, the insect escaped the firebreak?

To help pitch the eradication strategy, Michigan Senators Carl Levin and Debbie Stabenow requested that representatives from chemical companies also attend the Washington meeting with APHIS. Company representatives had approached the senators because they were angry that their company scientists had been excluded from the planning process. They argued that insecticides sold a legitimate resource to the EAB problem. They showed photographs of successfully treated trees.

The science panel, consisted mostly of academia, argued against the chemical company's participation, saying they would only confuse the issue. The science panel said pesticides are not capable of killing every single insect—a requirement—at least not safely. Since complete eradication was the goal, they claimed pesticides were not a viable option. They also claimed it would be far too expensive to treat the millions of trees necessary to do the job.

The chemical company representatives countered, "You don't know that, yet. At least give us a chance to find out how much it will cost."

The meeting was long and the meeting was contentious at times. Millions of dollars were at stake. APHIS is reported to have listened to all sides and at the end of the meeting determined: "We will study the proposal and let you know what we decide."

For months, APHIS weighed the plan. While they did, trees continued to die. The scouts reported the leading edge was expanding, and MDA inspectors discovered six new outbreaks beyond southeast Michigan, some of the locations as far away as Grand Rapids, Midland and East Lansing. These new outbreaks created disturbing implications to the proposed firebreak strategy.

To many people's astonishment, APHIS approved funding anyway, and they jumped into the fray with both feet.

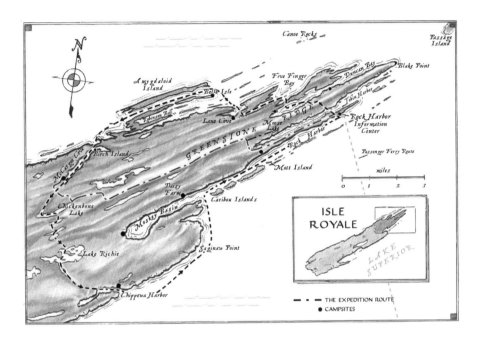

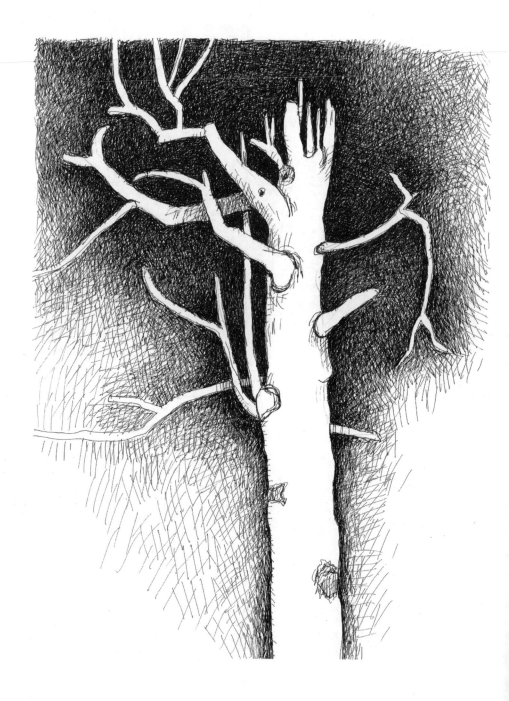

THE RIGHT BALANCE

"Nobody made a greater mistake than he who did nothing because he could do only a little."

~Edmund Burke

I WIPED DOWN THE BOTTOM OF THE CANOE, DRAGGED A PICNIC TABLE INTO THE sun and spread out every Hot-N-Tot, daredevil and spoon on top of the table. I examined each treble hook, sifted through every swivel-snap and leader, and even stripped off 20 feet of fishing line from the reels. I didn't see any evidence of spiny water fleas or zebra mussels.

This felt like no chore. Every fisherman loves to go through his tackle. The analogy has been made that a tackle box is full of lures no less shiny and no less colorful and covered in glitter than the fanciest jewelry draped in a jewelry box. However, cleaning the canoe and tackle was more than an opportunity to go through my "jewelry." It was my small attempt to protect wilderness. For unbeknownst to some worker in China, he had crated up trade-goods bound for the United States, oblivious to the fact that the crates were made of infested ash wood and that he was about to kill millions of trees. I was glad Ranger Carl had warned me. Cleaning my tackle meant I wouldn't be the person who wiped out an Isle Royale habitat.

It had taken a monumental effort to return Isle Royale to wilderness. Like much of the Upper Great Lakes Region, the island had been mined, logged, and trapped-out by the end of the 1800s. If not for the mining and logging companies tripping over themselves to sell their then unprofitable lands to the National Park Service in the 1920s, the island would look much different today. Even with the cessation of industry, it took 80 years of hard work and a dogged steadfastness by the Park Service to return the island to its current natural condition. That determination is embodied in all of the park's rules and regulations.

No pets are allowed on the island for fear they might spread disease-carrying fleas or ticks that could infect the wolves or other wildlife. (Unfortunately, a dog did slip into the island in the 1990s and canine-distemper was soon detected in some wolves, costing the lives of several.) Fishermen cannot bring live or cut bait onto inland lakes. No campfires are allowed except in designated fire pits. Off-trail hiking is discouraged and requires a permit. During the nesting seasons, visitors are to avoid any contact with nesting waterfowl and stay 100 yards away from loons. No feeding of the wildlife is allowed. No hunting is allowed. When visitors disembark off the passenger ferries or planes, they must go through orientation to listen to the above rules. They are not allowed off the dock until orientation is completed. All visitors—hikers, paddlers and boaters—must leave detailed itineraries with the rangers.

The many rules and regulations feel oppressive at times, but after witnessing the demise of so many ash trees, I can understand the park service's passion for rules and regs.

The National Park Service has done, and continues to do, a commendable job restoring and preserving wilderness areas. But I have noticed what I think are some harmless quirks. In 2002, Ranger Carl was wearing a sidearm. I asked him about the gun, and he said it was a new requirement since they are stationed on the border.

"The Canadian border?" I asked.

"Yes," he said. "You know, ever since 9/11."

Another quirk is the placement of garbage dumpsters. They are the first thing one sees—and smells—when arriving at the dock in Rock Harbor. It's not exactly the greatest first impression. The explanation for their location is the dumpsters need to be accessible for boats that take garbage to the mainland.

The Park Service does what it can, given the limited resources they have. They receive less money than they received ten years ago from the federal government, and any fight against invasive species often feels like trying to stop a tidal wave with a bailing can.

The Michigan Department of Agriculture certainly was struggling to stop the emerald ash borer. More and more outbreaks began to be reported. The primary quarantine area in southeast Michigan was growing. And researchers could not find any effective predators to feed on the insects.

The Animal and Plant Health Inspection Service (APHIS) approved funding for the already established scouting network. They provided monies for the Michigan Department of Agriculture (MDA) inspectors to enforce the quarantine of the seven infested counties in southeast Michigan. No shipment of ash trees or ash wood was allowed out of the quarantine zone. The scientists at Michigan State University were granted monies to research the nemesis. APHIS even approved the firebreak strategy, but wanted more details of how the MDA hoped to accomplish that.

With approval of funding, a handful of MDA inspectors began a paper-trail search for any ash trees that slipped outside of the quarantine zone by southeast Michigan nurseries that occurred prior to the quarantine going into effect. Going over sales records for the three previous years, they tracked one such sale to a west Michigan landscape company. The landscapers had planted six of the potentially infested ash trees in front of a Builders Square Store on the south side of Grand Rapids. When local inspectors examined the trees, all six were infested with the flat-headed, cream-colored emerald ash borer larvae.

The MDA decided to make a media event of removing the six trees. Our company was hired to do the removals.

Similar to the Detroit dental office gathering, a large group of local politicians, MDA inspectors, and Forest Service personnel gathered in the parking lot. Local TV stations set up remote broadcasting equipment. Reporters appeared and interviewed anyone who would talk with them. As company spokesperson for the tree service, I arrived early to talk with the press, and to keep the work area clear. I had warned our crew that they'd be working under a microscope.

When the crew arrived, they stepped out of their trucks, looked around the parking lot at all of the spectators and asked, "Where are the trees?"

I pointed to the six tiny trees they'd just walked by. None were taller than 10 feet. Accustomed to dealing with 80-foot oaks, Chris, the foreman, sarcastically whispered, "Think we can handle it?" As cameras swung our way, I suppressed a smile.

To ensure that we didn't alarm the insects of their impending doom, it was decided that one man would hold a tree upright while another cut it off at the ground. Two men would then carefully carry the ash upright over to the awaiting chipper. They would slowly tip the tree on its side and then shove it whole through the shredder. The inspectors donned hard hats and followed the crew's every step to see if any emerald-colored beetles flew off.

To remove the six trees took 10 minutes. The guys could have done it in two, but were asked to slow down so everybody could take pictures. Two crew members, Andy and Mark, stopped once to pose with a tree in-route to the shredder. The wood chips from the six trees barely dusted the bottom of the 20-yard truck.

We were instructed to cover the chips with a tarp and drive "the load" to a designated quarantined drop-off site in Detroit, which is a 100-mile journey. The transport of the chips and the return drive home took Andy six hours.

Besides wanting to make the public aware of the serious nature of the EAB problem, the other reason the MDA wanted the media event was to prepare the surrounding neighborhood for the removal of every ash tree within a mile radius of the store. Every single ash would go, no matter its location, size, or condition. This drastic measure was taken to ensure they eliminated any insects that may have already flown away and reproduced. The mile-radius area held approximately 100,000 ash trees.

Five other outlier sites in Michigan were dealt with in the same manner. Close to half a million Ash trees were removed. APHIS paid for it all. Before the last tree fell, ten more outlier sites were discovered.

The battle was going no better in southeast Michigan. Identifying where to place the firebreak ring proved near impossible. Even taking advantage of farm fields, lakes and any other non-ash tree covered lands, the cost projections for removing the ring of trees was astronomical. It cost about 10 million dollars to cut down the trees in the six outlier sites, an area totaling no larger than 30 square miles. How much would it cost to do 3,000 square miles? The EAB scouts, who continued to monitor the insects' progress, were seeing them travel alarming distances. If the cutting didn't take place soon, the ring would need to be expanded.

The Department of Agriculture put a good face on it all and held firm to their plan, but it was clear there was no stopping the emerald ash borer. It was also clear that if the MDA admitted defeat, APHIS would cut off their funding. The fate of the ash tree was looking bleak.

One segment of the war on EAB, however, was making progress. The entomologists at MSU were gaining insights about their foe. By simply offering different types of leaves and wood to the adult beetles and the larvae, they quickly learned that the emerald ash borer feeds strictly on ash (*Fraxinus*). In the beginning, a big fear was that the insect would attack other tree species, especially once the ash was all gone. Not an unreasonable concern.

Five years earlier in Chicago, a similar Asian pest had infiltrated the Windy City and that beetle had a taste for several tree species. One of its favorites was maple. An alert homeowner had seen a "weird bug" crawl out of her maple tree and placed the bug in an old pill bottle. She took it to the local garden center, who, in turn, took it to a city forester. A search of the department's reference books identified the insect as the Asian Long-Horned Beetle. Their reference books also noted that it was known to eat almost every deciduous tree species found in the Midwest, and was particularly fond of maples. Unlike Detroit, which had only one forester on staff, the City of Chicago has over 100—thanks largely to then Mayor Richard Daley's advocacy for trees.

The Chicago foresters went en-masse to the woman's home and scattered throughout the neighborhood. The team found a handful of beetles in adjacent trees.

Fortunately, the Asian Long-Horned Beetle can't fly. It crawls from tree to tree, making its containment much less challenging. As a result, the City of Chicago condemned every single tree within a 12 square-block area. They clear-cut the neighborhood.

The Asian Long-Horned Beetle was eradicated.

The Michigan Department of Agriculture often cited the Chicago project when justifying the emerald ash borer plan. It's why they drafted the firebreak ring. It was also why they decided to clear all of the ash trees within a mile of the Builders Square store.

For me, the Builders Square event came way too close to home. I was hoping the battle would remain in the Detroit area—some 100 miles away—and, with the removal of the Grand Rapids trees, I could return to my normal tree-doctoring duties. And things did return to normal, but not for long. Two months later, I got a call from Steve Snell, the arborist at Grand Valley State University.

The insect's paper trail had also led inspectors to seven ash trees planted at the Allendale Campus. The university is only 10 miles west of Grand Rapids and GVSU is far and away my biggest tree care client. Over 20,000 students attend the university, and the campus has a youthful energy and buzz that reminds me of my college days. To care for their trees was and is a responsibility I take very seriously.

The MDA inspectors found EAB exit holes in the trunks of three of the planted ash trees. The adult beetle creates a distinctive D-shaped exit hole. The inspectors removed the three trees and autopsied them. No actual insects were found, but the evidence clearly indicated that the trees had been infested. Inspectors fanned out to search nearby ash trees, but didn't find a single beetle or larva.

At that time, I'd been helping to care for the university's trees for 15 years. Early in the school's history, it was nicknamed, "Grass Valley," not for what the name may bring to mind, but rather due to its scarcity of trees and abundance of turf. The campus is practically forested now and has won several national landscape awards. Unfortunately for the university, over 50 percent of their shade trees, at the time, were ash. This battle wasn't close to home. It was sitting at my kitchen table.

The MDA didn't know what to do. Legally, they couldn't condemn ash trees without finding any actual insects. Symptoms alone were not enough to order removals. Unless ordered to, the university wasn't about to remove half the trees on campus.

A meeting was held to discuss the situation. Sitting in the conference room were university deans, township and county officials, local extension agents, soil conservation foresters, the grounds' manager, the GVSU arborist and … me. The MDA went through their usual EAB presentation. They showed pictures of the insect's current whereabouts, explained the insect's lifecycle, or as much of it as they knew at the time, and used reams of maps and graphs to illustrate their eradication strategy.

I kept thinking during their hour-long presentation that they could benefit from learning some marketing skills. The lecture was well-intentioned, but had the net effect of boring an audience into a stupor. I dozed through the first 45 minutes, so I'd be alert for the bad news when it came. It finally did, delivered in the usual flat monotone.

"...when we find an emerald ash borer, we will remove all of your ash trees."

I immediately raised my hand to ask a question. It was the first one of the afternoon. "Does that mean if you don't find any insects, you won't remove any trees?"

"Well, yes, though it's only a matter of time..." the speaker said, surprised at the question.

"But..." I interjected, "until then—no borers—no tree removals."

"That's right."

The speaker moved on. But I had what I wanted. I turned and looked at Mr. Snell, the university arborist. He nodded, and glanced away. We said no more at the meeting.

The MSU entomologists had learned that the emerald ash borer feeds strictly on ash trees. It was an easy lab experiment to run and test results were immediate. They were also testing various insecticides. When several products worked, they went from their labs to the streets of Detroit to test them on real trees.

The researchers treated several hundred ash, and then waited two, four, and eight weeks before removing the trees to examine them. Once cut down, they peeled off the bark and counted the dead and/or live insects inside. Two months following the street tree assessment, a report was released detailing the results.

Within days, there were commercials airing on television, radio and in the newspapers about "the cure" for the emerald ash borer. The companies that sold the more successful (and less successful) insecticides used the report to full advantage, citing the study for credibility. At my office, we received brochures from several chemical companies. The speed of the commercial response to the university report was a lesson the researchers never forgot. All later reports were carefully screened and any implication of product preference was removed. Future studies were more technical and data-oriented, and eliminated phrases like "tremendous knock down" or "killed them all."

The success rate for one particular insecticide stood out. The active ingredient is Imidacloprid, and is sold under several product names. It is in a class of pesticides known as the neonictoids and, as the name suggests, is a derivative of nicotine. The Third Edition of *Webster's Dictionary* defines *nicotine* not merely as a by-product of tobacco, but as "...a poisonous, water-soluble alkaloid, $C_{10}H_{14}N_2$, found in tobacco leaves and used, ordinarily in aqueous solution of its sulfate, as an insecticide." Some companies claim neonictoids are natural pesticides since they're derived from a plant. That's a pretty loose use of the word, "natural," since typically a few extra chemicals are added to enhance the products. But I can vouch for Imidacloprid's effectiveness, having prescribed it for pine borers, bronze birch borers and several other native destructive borer insects. My opinion is that pesticides are a necessary evil in urban environments where there is little to no predator—prey balance remaining. Used judiciously, with much emphasis on the word, judicious, the benefits of insecticides can sometimes outweigh the consequences of non-use. It is one of those risk—benefit questions a conscientious professional constantly should ask themselves.

One advantage of Imidacloprid is it can be applied either as a soil drench or directly into the tree as a trunk injection. Soil drenches and trunk injections reduce pesticide drift that occurs when trees are sprayed. Since borers feed beneath the bark in the sapwood, to reach the insect the pesticides must either be absorbed by the tree's roots or introduced directly into the sap-stream. By lacing tree sap with Imidacloprid, the material is transported directly to the insect.

Putting aside the environmental and human health issues, (not recommended, of course) pesticide applications are also expensive. Although homeowners can buy diluted, less expensive versions of Imidacloprid over the counter, it isn't just the cost of the product that presents problems for the public. People also need to purchase the tools to apply it and the knowledge to do so appropriately. Treatments also need to be repeated every year until the trees are no longer in danger, a point in time that even the experts can't predict. While some residents may find the cost acceptable, many more did not. In cash-strapped Detroit, the city's forestry department certainly could not afford to treat hundreds of thousands of ash trees.

The arborist at Grand Valley and I had already discussed our strategy prior to walking into the meeting. By this time, it was becoming increasingly clear that the eradication strategy was failing. There were 10 additional outlier sites that needed cutting, and it had already cost millions to clear the first six sites. The emerald ash borer had also penetrated beyond the first proposed firebreak around southeast Michigan. We felt if we could stall long enough at Grand Valley, there was a strong possibility the requirement to remove outlier trees would be lifted.

I said to Steve, "We just need to be sure the inspectors don't find any insects on campus until they lift the tree removal edict. If we can wait them out, I think we can save them."

Steve said, "Get me a price to treat every tree on campus. Also, Vic, keep this to yourself."

"Why?"

"Not everyone at the university will think pesticides are a viable option. If this gets out, we're done."

I kept quiet.

One month later, we treated every tree on campus. We treated them again the next year and the next. No emerald ash borers were found at Grand Valley for four years—two years after the demise of the eradication strategy.

Whether our success was due to the effectiveness of the treatments or because there were no emerald ash borers to begin with, we'll never know. Ten years later, the emerald ash borer swept through campus, as it has through the rest of West Michigan. The university's current policy is to treat only those trees they deem necessary to maintain the arbor-effect along Campus Drive. The rest of the ash are being replaced as they die-off.

The too-late diagnosis, the lack of firsthand knowledge of their foe, and failure to find an effective predator eventually proved to be fatal to the EAB war. Several factors played a role:

- It was mistakenly believed that the insect first arrived in Detroit about five years prior to its discovery, and that the scouts had pinpointed its whereabouts. In fact, they now believe it had arrived some ten years before that.
- The six-mile-wide firebreak ring was proposed because it was erroneously believed that the emerald ash borer couldn't migrate farther than six miles in a year's time. It's still unclear today how far the beetle can fly.
- It was also mistakenly believed that the insect's location was limited to southeast Michigan, which it clearly was not.

The MDA eventually dropped the idea of creating a firebreak around southeast Michigan. They also dropped the outlier tree removal program. The insect was simply spreading too fast for them to contain and the panel of experts finally admitted the plan was unworkable. Although at one point there was actually some serious discussion about moving the proposed firebreak from around southeast Michigan to the State's south border—cutting down ash trees all the way from Lake Erie to Lake Michigan along the border between Indiana, Ohio and Michigan, using the Great Lakes as a natural firebreak. The plan would have meant sacrificing every ash tree in the Lower Peninsula of Michigan. And while some experts felt such a plan was worth the sacrifice if it meant stopping EAB's spread across the continent, the idea was eventually scrapped.

When emerald ash borers began to show up in Ohio, Indiana, and one small outbreak in North Carolina, the panel gave up the firebreak strategy for good.

Today, millions of ash trees have died throughout the Midwest, and no cure is in sight. Researchers are still searching for that predator that will feed on EAB, and establish a predator - prey balance. During the early stages of the crisis, scientists were dispatched to China to see if they could locate an insect, bird or fungus that keeps the Chinese emerald ash borer in check. But even with the best of intentions, introducing new species as a method of eradication is risky. What else might that predator feed on? It takes several years to adequately test the impact an introduced species might make.

Unfortunately for the American scientists, the one Chinese entomologist who specialized in emerald ash borers was hinted to be in hiding or under arrest. According to one of the lead U.S. researchers, who asked to remain unnamed, the Chinese officials won't or can't say where their entomologist is. The scientist is rumored to have anti-government feelings. He still hasn't been found.

For homeowners dealing with only one or two ash trees, more effective insecticides were later discovered by the MSU entomologists, who continue to do research. A single application of a product called Tree-age®, with an active ingredient of Emmimectin benzoate, provides up to three years of control. Discovering a product that persists within a tree for more than one year was an unexpected benefit from the program. Tree-age is the only insecticide known to persist in the sapwood for more than one year. It seriously reduces the number of applications needed to control EAB. But Tree-age must be applied by certified pesticide applicators, and repeated every two-to-three years. The labor and expertise necessary to apply Tree-age makes the treatment relatively expensive, though when the cost is spread over three years, it is not as stinging. On a per tree basis, Tree-age is a great product. As a forest-wide remedy, the cost still makes it unworkable as an eradication strategy.

With the arrival of the emerald ash borer to Detroit, another North American predator-prey balance is thrown irreversibly into a tailspin. One more ecological balance that took centuries to reach is destroyed, and a continent of ash trees is likely to die as a result.

In an effort to deal with the loss of my blue-collar, hometown trees, I tried to look at the loss objectively. I could take issue with the words "invasive" or "introduced." Only humans draw habitat lines and determine what's native and what's not. Given enough time, habitats evolve, and the plants and animals that dwell inside those habitats shift with them. If I could go back 15,000 years, a mere blink of geological time, Isle Royale would be covered by glaciers. The island would be considered an arctic habitat. Ash trees probably didn't call Detroit home until 10,000 years ago.

Natural disasters can have the same effect as an invasive species. They are considered "natural." A flood, volcano or forest fire can wipe out species overnight. What makes an exotic green beetle any different?

My arguments, however, didn't help me much. The logic sounded hollow. My rationalizations sounded for what they were—rationalizations.

In Grand Rapids, Michigan, I service Siberian elms, Norway maples and Austrian pines. Colorado spruce, Korean dogwoods, and Kwazan cherries are under my care. The trees are all introduced species. They can't create a forest. They couldn't even grow into a small woodlot. The land where they live is now a jumbled clutter of confused trees, of misguided understory plants and grasses that don't belong. The plants are indentured to a foreign land. The grasses are wild, but only in the sense that the seed blows in from neighboring lawns.

The predator - prey balances that once kept so many of our trees healthy are now non-existent, and the imbalance calls for emergency actions. My work often consists of treating native trees for non-native pests ... or ... treating non-native trees for native pests.

A WILDERNESS VENTURE

"It is better to know some of the questions than all of the answers."

~James Thurber

BETWEEN MY JUNIOR AND SENIOR YEARS AT COLLEGE, I WORKED AT A CHEVY PLANT. My sister's, boyfriend's, father got me the job. His dad was the plant manager and in those days a person had to know somebody to be interviewed, let alone hired. As big brothers do, I remember kidding my sister that she'd finally picked a good boyfriend, which turned out to be truer than I knew. They would later marry and raise three wonderful children.

The factory job would provide me with two long-term benefits. The first one was the wages. The auto industry in Detroit was humming in the mid-70s. Three shifts worked around the clock, seven days a week. Being a new hire, they placed me on third shift, which paid a ten percent premium. Thanks to the UAW, Saturdays paid double-time. Sundays paid triple-time. In one summer, I earned enough money to pay for my last year of college and, with help from Dad, graduate debt free.

The second benefit proved to be far more valuable.

My particular job entailed unloading rack after rack of freshly chromed bumpers and hanging them onto hooks connected to conveyors. The conveyors carried the bumpers to the next dipping station. Everywhere I looked, I saw wet, gleaming bumpers weaving through the plant as if trapped in a maze. The shiny chrome could double as mirrors and looked eerily out of place in the dim, dusty factory that stunk of sulfur and chromium and seemed to ooze hot grease out of every crevice.

I punched out of work at seven each morning, leaving the factory with the pound of heavy machinery ringing in my ears and the taste of metallic grit, which lasted long after I went home. The chemical stench clung to my clothes so badly that my mother wouldn't let me inside the house, leaving a change of clothes hanging in the garage.

Working through the night, performing the same menial task over and over again, with little else to occupy my thoughts, I liked to picture where all the bumpers escape to—the lucky ones—the bumpers that now roam free with their vehicles. As I left the factory each morning, I would stand for a moment at the cavernous opening of the "plant" (strange choice of name) to watch the sunrise. Pausing to take in the new day, I would feel an almost uncontrollable urge to walk down to Newburgh Road, stick out my thumb for a ride north and not stop until I ran out of rides, or better yet, out of roads. It was while working that summer job that I made a commitment to find a career working outdoors.

Some old high school friends disagreed about the decision. They argued that leaving the factory with its union scale wages and great fringe benefits to work somewhere outdoors was hardly an upward career move. All I could tell them in reply was the old-timers at the factory told me they'd beat me silly if they saw me return next summer after getting a college degree.

The liberal arts degree I'd earned proved to be of little help for acquiring decent paying work, and was no help at all with finding work outdoors. What I lacked in salary I had to make up in hours worked. After graduation from college I went through a series of painful jobs—sorting stones on a rock crusher, cutting rear ends out of cars for scrap metal in salvage yards, managing a discount garden center and then working for a lawn care service. To this day, the smell of broadleaf weed killer makes me nauseous.

Unable to stomach another season of spraying lawns, I answered an ad in the newspaper to sell tree care. The one thing the liberal arts degree had provided me was a skill for communicating—written and oral. I'm not sure, but my last name may have lent me some perceived credibility. Whatever the reason, the owners decided I might make a good arborist. Thirty years later, it's the job I still do today.

Since clients can't bring their sick trees to me, I spend much of my work days traveling southwest Michigan. At each stop, I walk a homeowner's yard, a city park or a farmer's woodlot, helping them grow healthier trees. Southwest Michigan is dotted with hard-working communities that are surrounded by a patchwork of woods and farmlands. Along its western border is Lake Michigan, a deep blue marvel, its shore fringed with some of the largest freshwater sand dunes in the world. This unique mix of urban, farm and lakeside habitats contain a broad range of tree species and an interesting and diverse group of people. I rarely see the same problem—tree or human—twice in the same day.

Before the Europeans arrived to Michigan, the entire state was forested, minus a few plots of oak savanna, a trace of prairie land and a small handful of burned-over tracts. The state was clear-cut by the late 1800s. Most of the re-growth has been cut again.

The land keeps attempting to recreate those forests. That's not happening of course. We keep intervening and, as a result, the trees in Michigan, throughout the Midwest and throughout much of the country for that matter, are now a checkerboard of third and fourth growth and introduced species. Trees are still being harvested on a regular basis, not only for timber, but for pulpwood to meet our burgeoning need for paper products. Trees are also cleared for new developments and a surprising number are cut for firewood. There's little-to-no chance the land will see old growth forests anytime soon.

In the cities, some of the trees are pushing 80 years old, and many of them need to be replaced. They've declined in health to a point where they've become a danger. City trees die young. Their urban habitats aren't conducive to encouraging old age. They rarely live 100 years. Judging by the pictures of the logging camps from the 1800s, the trees I see bear pale resemblance to the mammoth pinewoods and hardwoods that once graced the region. Those two-to-three-hundred-year-old monarchs would call my eighty-year-old trees youngsters.

Traveling the countryside, making my rounds, I see trees sprouting on any land that's left fallow for more than a couple of years. Michigan was meant to grow trees and there's no lack of work for an arborist. I am convinced that if we quit plowing our fields and mowing our lawns, the state would be covered in forests in less than a century.

Working as an arborist has satisfied my desire to be outdoors—but not completely. Vacations spent near the lakes and forests of upper Michigan also help. Yet over the ensuing years, and much like that summer at the auto plant, I began finding myself daydreaming of wandering the Northwoods. While examining a linden tree in a client's yard, a gust of wind would rustle the leaves and I'd forget why I was there. While walking a woodlot, I'd come across a game-trail and begin to follow it. It was when these "drifting-off" episodes began occurring more and more often, the urge to wander increasingly intense that I decided to allow myself a month to explore a real wilderness. The wilderness I chose was Isle Royale. The time I picked to go was over my fiftieth birthday.

When I told friends of my pending month-long sojourn, several questioned. "Are you having a mid-life crisis? Are you looking to reassess your life? How can you afford to take that much time off from work?" Some even asked, "Are you having problems at home?" To which I quickly answered, "No." Neither my wife nor the owners of the tree service objected to the extended leave.

My more religious friends sighed as if they understood, and said, "Good idea. Time to draw closer to God."

"I hope so," I would reply, and meant it. But that wasn't the primary reason I went.

The real reason was I went there to explore. I simply wanted some time to wander with no particular purpose or agenda. Isle Royale has no roads, no industry, no smog and the wildlife behaves like wildlife. There's no taste of chlorine in the water, no cattle grazing inside barbed-wire lands, no corn fields with naked-soiled furrows. You can't hear a single car engine.

And Isle Royale National Park is about as wild and remote a place as can be found east of the Mississippi. Located in the northwest portion of Lake Superior, Isle Royale is closer to Canada than to the U.S. The park itself is an archipelago of over 400 smaller islands that surround the main island. The main island is 48 miles long and 8 miles wide.

Isle Royale is a federally designated wilderness area. It is touted by the National Park Service as the least-visited National Park in the lower forty-eight states. No motorized vehicles are allowed. Isle Royale is reached only by seaplane or boat. The park is so pristine that in 1981 the United Nations declared Isle Royale an International Biosphere Preserve, a Hall of Fame designation for environmentally important sites.

Vernon Krueger, the late world-renowned canoeist, was asked at a forestry convention I attended, "Where was the most beautiful place you ever canoed?" Mr. Krueger had paddled every continent. He'd made a career out of chronicling his journeys. He'd seen countless mountain streams, wilderness lakes and coastlines. He once paddled the entire length of North and South America. He didn't paddle down the East or West Coast. He canoed through the two continents.

The place that left the biggest impression?

"Lake Superior," he answered.

"It wasn't its size," he said. "There's something about the light, something about the water. Lake Superior does something to you, not sure what." Standing behind the podium and clearly struggling to express what he felt, he eventually shrugged and left us with, "There was just something about the light."

Mr. Krueger is not alone in his opinion of the region. From the current park rangers, to the early settlers, to the Jesuit priests and voyageurs before them, including the Native Americans who never left its shores—all have lauded the vitality of the Lake Superior region. It begs the question. What is so special about this place? Is there a technical explanation? Given the area's brutal winters, its mosquito hatches of Biblical proportions, and its rugged terrain, why does a lungful of air there make a person feel like Hiawatha? What is it about this place that makes me feel like I, too, could travel the length of the lake in only three paddle strokes?

As I was to learn, there was, indeed, an explanation. I always thought of Isle Royale as strictly a place for outdoor enthusiasts. I thought of the island as a closely guarded wilderness area that park rangers patrol. I thought of it as *wilderness extremis*. I discovered the island is far more than that. It wasn't until I looked into Isle Royale's history in preparation for my trip that I learned a host of scientists work there. It turns out the park has a dual purpose. Due to its isolation and pristine nature, the island is a laboratory for studying an untainted environment. With its Great-Lake-sized moat protecting it, the island barely feels man's influence. The island is, in essence, the control subject for several important environmental studies.

According to the Isle Royale Research Institute, more than 2,500 research papers refer to the scientific studies performed on the island. The Isle Royale Research Institute (IRRI) is more of an organization than a school or an institute. Started by Dr. Ken Vrana, a noted limnologist and Great Lakes underwater explorer, the IRRI electronically collects research papers pertaining to Isle Royale and the Lake Superior basin. Their files offer scientists a way to obtain up-to-date information on current and past projects. The Institute sends grant requests. It also provides an information conduit for the two universities— Michigan Tech and the University of Minnesota at Duluth—which employ most of the island's researchers.

Many of the science papers refer to Isle Royale's 50-plus year predator-prey study of wolves and moose. But there are many other subjects covered. Some papers are written for the general public, others for small groups of scientists. "Temperature Dynamics in Dimictic Lakes" and "Moose Teeth as Monitors of Environmental Isotopic Parameters" probably won't ever be published in *National Geographic* or *Discover* magazines, but "The Lives and Loves of Some Sly Fox" might.

Some scientists monitor the Tobin Harbor brook trout—a trout indigenous only to Isle Royale. Some map raptor migratory routes and nesting sites. Others monitor the common loon's chick hatch rates. Wildlife scientists study the habits of the wolves and moose, but they also cover the predator–prey relationship between the red fox and snowshoe hare. They study the connection between ravens and wolves, too. The wildlife people suspect the ravens may lead the packs to moose, and if not, the ravens do harass sleeping wolves to wake them, presumably so they will go hunting. The ravens scavenge the moose remains from their kills.

Unfortunately, a few invasive species have reached the island's coastal waters. Marine biologists are monitoring the "progress" of the spiny water flea and zebra mussel. Both are imports from Eastern Europe. Others monitor the earthworms' movements on the island, which are not native to the island. Scientists take beaver counts, otter counts and study the habits of merlins – a small falcon. They investigate mosses and lichen and the micro-biology of the inland lakes.

The wolf-moose study garners most of the public's attention. But in my opinion, the air and water quality research may be the island's most important projects. Researchers take sediment cores from the bottom of Siskiwit and Sargent Lakes. The sediment layers provide annual levels of toxins that go back several centuries. With no island industry to taint the water since the early 1900s, the only way for certain toxins to reach the inland lakes is on the prevailing winds. The findings helped to justify the ban of leaded gasoline, DDT and PCBs. We can thank Isle Royale, in part, for the Clean Air Act.

From the top of the old fire tower on Mount Ojibwa, one can see up and down the length of the island. You can see Canada to the north and on clear days just make out the tip of Michigan's Keweenaw Peninsula to the south, fifty miles away. The fire tower now serves as a raised platform for climate scientists. They mount air filters on the tower, and I'm told, filters test for pollutants down to parts per billion, and that the transponders send data to orbiting satellites, which in turn relay the information to waiting scientists—or more likely research assistants—sitting in labs back on the mainland. All of that equipment is meant to chronicle the pristine, to gauge clean, to evaluate air dirtied only by distant smoke stacks.

In the days when the fire towers were manned by lookouts, and prior to the island becoming a National Park, the island's resort owners advertised the air as capable of healing maladies ranging from asthma to croup to hay fever. "Invigorating" is the word most often used from that era to describe an Isle Royale vacation. Advertisements boasted, "Trout so thick, they jump in your boat." "Water so clean as to purify the blood." "Air so refreshing, it heals the most wearied of souls."

I'd have a hard time arguing their hyperbole. I'm not sure about a cure for hay fever, but I do know that after spending a couple of days on the island I feel stronger. Maybe it's being outdoors day and night, maybe it's all of the exercise, but more than once, I've commented to campers I meet, how alive I feel. No one I've met disagrees, and that's despite feeling unwashed, tired, and sore.

I am particularly interested by how island researchers use indicator plants to study air quality. Lichen, I learned, is ideal for the job. It is the terrestrial version of coral reefs. Lichen, much like the mosses they're often confused with, take moisture and nutrients from the surrounding air. Lichen has annual growth rings, which if left undisturbed, scientists can use to collect water and air data that go back many decades. They can crosscheck those findings against the lake's sediment samples. And Isle Royale is a great place to study lichen. The place is covered with them. Lichen grows on the rocks. It grows up and down tree trunks. It hangs in long curtained wisps from branches. I'm constantly wiping the wisps off my face.

Part of my interest in the lichen is that they also provide me with work. I am, on occasion, called to diagnose trees in Southwest Michigan that customers describe as "breaking out in a rash." Fortunately, it is only crusty patches of lichen taking up residence on the bark of their trees. It's a nice house-call to make. For once, I can tell a homeowner there's nothing wrong. Lichens pose no threat. They just use the bark for something to attach to.

Talking with the researchers on Isle Royale, they impress me with their patience. Their work takes many years to complete, and, as any of them will tell you, there's no thrill to tweezing through wolf scat or counting *E Coli* numbers in a drop of water. The researchers explain it takes a long time to gather good samples. It takes them more time for the samples to be properly analyzed and trends noted. The data needs to be sorted, organized and recorded on corresponding tables, graphs and charts. The reports must be peer reviewed and, if approved, the reports are rewritten in a manner that laymen can understand. It takes more time yet for people of influence to read the reports and some more time to legislate change.

Learning about how Isle Royale played such an important scientific role was an unexpected bonus to my wilderness venture.

The scientists also taught me that to fully appreciate places like Isle Royale, a person needs to think like they do. Be patient. I discovered it takes time to explore properly. You need to slow down enough to notice the details. And slowing down was something I doubt I could have done without the island's help or the extended stay. The weather dictates what one can do here, especially when travelling on the water in a canoe. After arriving, it quickly became clear that it was best not to follow a schedule. The island has its own timetable. Without those dictates, I might have missed much of what I was about to experience.

The scientists also explained why Isle Royale is so invigorating. By definition, a wilderness area is clean. There may be no hospital staff scrubbing the place down and it's certainly not antiseptic, especially with over 1,000 moose on the island. I seldom saw them, but there's ample evidence they're here. They leave broad horse-size hoof prints. They defecate wherever they want. Countless other animals and birds do the same. Insects are everywhere. The ground is covered with decaying feces and organic matter. A cubic foot of soil contains thousands of organisms when measured at the microscopic level. Ironically, all of that thriving biomass creates the healthiest of environments.

I didn't know it at the time, but part of the reason I chose Isle Royale for a sabbatical was I was seeking a land unchanged, a countryside unaltered, and native habitats that are still intact. After years of explaining to thousands of people how their trees are suffering due to the harsh and sometimes sterile growing conditions we ask them to endure, I had grown callous. After awhile you grow a little numb.

I no longer paid much attention to all of the environmental warnings. I confess I was weary of hearing about habitat losses—despite the tragic reality of those losses. It's difficult to pick up an outdoor magazine, a science journal or even a newspaper and not find an article that doesn't end with a plea to write your congressman or urge you to make a difference. When I came across those pleas, I skimmed through those passages.

Ironically, it wasn't the scent of early-morning smog blurring the skyline of Grand Rapids that reminded me the world has changed. It wasn't even when seeing thousands of ash trees die that I felt an ill-wind approaching. No, it was while paddling a remote wilderness lake.

One September morning the year prior to the Isle Royale trip, I was traveling from Grand Rapids to Southeast Michigan to attend a tree care conference. I was driving alone, and normally when alone in the car, I listen to the radio. For some reason that morning, I didn't and during the two-hour drive was completely unaware of the dreadful events of that day. The skies were clear in southern Michigan, as they were over New York City. There wasn't a single cloud in the sky, not even contrails. The sky was so remarkably blue it caught my attention. In route, I leaned out of the truck window several times to get a broader view.

I arrived at the conference around 11 a.m. Instead of attendees sitting through workshops or participating in training sessions, everybody was crowded around a small television set that one of the vendors had brought. I found Bob Kelly, a co-worker from the tree service, and asked him, "What's going on?" He took me aside and explained. Bob was visibly shaken.

Almost a hundred men and women were silently watching the news replay one jet and then a second smashing into the Twin Towers, the towers eventually crumpling to the ground. We would find out later that except for military aircraft, all commercial and private planes had been ordered to land. For a few brief hours, the skies had literally cleared over North America. When I heard the news about the aircraft, I shook my head at what a price we paid to make the sky so blue.

One year later, I'm floating stone-still in a canoe on Lake LaSage, deep in Isle Royale's backcountry, and two weeks into my month's stay. It's a windless, quiet day. I'd stopped paddling for a moment and the wooden minnow I'm fishing floats to the surface and lies motionless. The monofilament line rests atop the glassed water in lazy sweeps creating tiny furrows in the lake's skin.

Taking a deep breath, I inhale cool, clean, damp air.

I pick up the paddle and push on. The lure submerges. The line disappears beneath the surface. The sploosh and gurgle of a working paddle returns. Bow waves spread behind me.

I don't think of it for a few seconds because I'd been on the island long enough now to almost forget about such things. The shimmering green forest reflected off the glassed lake would make a perfect screen saver. I winced, not because of any isolation I felt but because the scene brought to mind a virtual picture.

The day would be the most difficult day of the month's hiatus. It would require a Herculean effort to cross the island alone from McCargo Cove to Chippewa Harbor with all of my packs and the canoe. I shouldn't dally. But somehow it didn't feel right to rip across this beautiful lake as if trying to beat rush hour.

I slowed and stopped again. I laid the paddle across my knees and leaned back, laying my head on the stern of the canoe. Water dribbled from the paddle. The drops slowed and then stopped.

All was silent. But for a few dragonflies in flight, nothing moved.

Not a single cottage breaks the shoreline. No aerial towers breach the horizon. The barely ruffled water reflected a blurred land softened further by mosses and ferns and lichen.

I stare up at the sky, and see three different jets inching across a pale-blue sky, leaving snow-white contrails as they go. The jets were the only sign of civilization. Ten other jets must have recently passed. The older contrails were slowly dissolving. The streaks are of varying widths and lengths and stages of dissipation. Ironically, and sadly, it is as clear a sky as I've ever seen on Isle Royale. Even at night, the blink of wing lights and the steady glow of orbiting satellites are never absent.

Only once have I ever seen a perfectly clear sky.

ALL ALONE

"I read there that all things live by a generous power and dance to a mighty tune; or I read there that all things are scattered and hurled, ..."

~Annie Dillard

REACHING THE SOUTH SHORE IN A SINGLE DAY FROM MCCARGO COVE HAD ALWAYS BEEN part of the plan. Even at age fifty, there was enough of the expeditioner in me to see if I could still do it. Ten years earlier, Ken and I had made a similar island crossing, and it had nearly done us in. We were so tired by the time we reached Malone Bay from McCargo that we didn't bother with dinner and went straight to bed.

It's eight miles from McCargo Cove to Chippewa Harbor as the crow flies. But the winding trails and multiple portages between each of the four inland lakes make the distance four times that far. I'd been reasonable about the rest of my island travelling, not risking anything farther than paddling six-to-ten miles per day or portaging for more than a mile. You need to treat a month on Isle Royale as a marathon, not a sprint.

I did make it to Chippewa Harbor...but just barely. Most of my gear, however, did not.

I'd run out of daylight, which was just as well. I couldn't have walked another step. My feet were so raw and blistered by the time I made the last portage between Lake Richie and Chippewa Lake that I left a litter of paddles and packs along the trail and even left the canoe behind at Lake Richie. I managed to drag my sleeping bag and a light day-pack into the campground at dusk. I dropped the pack like a sack of rocks on the floor of the shelter before unrolling the bag to crash.

As I soaked my feet in the lake the next morning, every single muscle ached. Fortunately, I had the next several days to recover, and would need them.

With half of the month's sabbatical behind me, I'd needed to take stock on where things stood.

My supplies looked good. I was on schedule as I'd rationed out my daily provisions as planned. If I kept to my schedule, the food and fuel should also make it to the end of the month. But for my blistered feet, my body was holding up well, too. I was terribly sore, but knew I'd heal in a couple of days with some rest and some moleskin to the blisters. With that said, psychologically, I was feeling strange, or more accurately, different.

For the past two weeks, I'd answered no phone calls, watched no television, nor listened to a radio. I never once checked email. The few conversations I had were held face-to-face and in real time. The only motors I heard were the occasional boat or the distant growl of an ore freighter. Jets traveled overhead, but were too high to be heard. Once or twice a day, I would notice the drone of an airplane. The sound was rare enough to cause me to look up.

While I was soaking my feet and contemplating my situation, the water taxi arrived at the dock. I heard its engines before seeing the ferry turn into the channel. Four groups of campers got off. They all hustled away to secure a shelter, pausing only long enough to say, "Hi," and ask where I was from. Dangling my feet in the lake, I could hear the shelter doors squeak open and close. I heard packs unzipped, clothes and supplies sorted, stoves pumped and lit, excited conversation. It seemed the new arrivals were in a hurry. I shrugged. Everyone's like that the first couple of days on the island.

I dried my feet, threw on my boots and decided I'd better ginger-foot it down the trail to Lake Richie to retrieve my gear and canoe. When I returned, the campers were all gone, evidently bustling away to begin their treks. I didn't see anyone else for five days. Not even a kayaker paddled through. As it was getting toward the end of September, when the weather cools and students are back in school, park visitation dwindles. Toward the end of the season—the park closes in early October—it's not uncommon to be the only person in the more distant campgrounds such as Chippewa Harbor.

Though five days may not seem that long to be completely alone, I'd never done it before. The seclusion took my already two-week old wilderness-heightened senses to an even higher level. If a twig snapped or a fish jumped in the bay, it made me jump. My peripheral vision expanded, too. An odd shake of a leaf at the edge of sight caught my attention. The way a branch bounced signaled a gray jay had taken flight, not a chickadee. It was a depth of recognition and alertness I'd never possessed before.

All of my senses grew more acute. More than that, they went on high alert. Every sight, sound and smell etched itself into my memory. By the fourth day of solitude, that sensitivity reached a crescendo.

I was fishing the big lake, canoeing along the south shore of the main island, just west of Saginaw Point. From that off-shore position, I could see up and down the coast. Isle Royale rose before me, its green flank rising from the water. The sun beat down on shore, baking the rocks just above the water-line, so that even at a hundred feet away, I could feel heat radiate off the exposed stone. The trees above, up the hillside, wafted an aroma of soggy earth, damp cedar, and decaying aspen leaves. The clean air permeated every breath.

In the other three directions—east, south, and west—Lake Superior's wrinkled blue skin spread to the horizon. It was a slightly hazy day and the sky held no seam or blemish to it. The sky was one continuous cream-tinted blue that blurred at the horizon. No boat could be seen on the lake and no aircraft flew low enough to appear through the haze. The riffled waves clipped a quick metallic ping against the side of the aluminum hull, and I noticed each creak the old Smoker Craft made as it bent to its task. The dip of the paddle was a half-smack, half-sploosh. Every single sensation clearly registered in my brain for what each sight, sound and smell were.

Fishing was slow all morning. I had tried several different lures. None of them had enticed more than a couple of strikes all day. Fortunately, just before dark, a lake trout slammed the spoon I dragged behind the canoe. The violent jerk on the rod startled me so much I almost dropped the paddle in the lake. Gathering my wits, I reeled the fish up, reached down, and snatched it out of the water. The fish wriggled like a mad thing. I gripped him for dear life for I was clinging to dinner. Taking-up the needle-nose pliers that were tied to a strut, I unhooked the trout and placed him on a stringer.

The sun had set by the time I arrived back at camp, but there was enough light to clean the fish by, using the canoe paddle as a cutting board. I then gently wrapped the two filets in fern leaves. When done, I carried the filets up to the shelter and set them inside to protect my dinner from the camp fox that had a nose for any food left unattended. Walking back down to the water, I pulled the canoe all the way up on shore and flipped it over to keep any rain out during the night. I cleaned my knife and rinsed the paddle off. Standing there, silently taking in the harbor, I listened to twilight as it gathered across the harbor. The songbirds were settling into the trees to roost. A pair of loons sang somewhere out on the lake and a gentle breeze sifted through needled boughs. I sighed with content, turned and said goodnight to the lake, walking the path up to the shelter.

It was time to make dinner.

Inside the shelter, I pumped the plunger on the fuel bottle to pressurize it and lit the stove. I then poured a cup of rice into a sauce pan filled with water. Minute rice is a wonderful camp dish. It's so easy to make. If you're hungry—and you're always hungry—the thought of a little salt and a pat of butter melting over a mound of steaming rice will make your stomach growl.

When the rice was cooked, I placed the lid on the sauce pan and set it aside. I replaced it with a frying pan, spooned some Crisco into the center, and waited for the oil to melt into a puddle. Retrieving the fillets, I picked off bits of fern and dusted the fillets with breading. The oil was already hot. The wet fish popped and spat as I laid it in the pan. Soon the aroma of fried fish filled the shelter.

Five minutes later, I plied the steaming rice on a plate, knifed the butter onto the top of it and laid the fish over that. Fork and knife in hand, I dug in.

After dinner, in the beam of my head lamp, I cleaned the dishes down at the lake. It was fully dark now, but clear and the stars were brilliant. The haze of that day had dissipated. Once the chores were finished, I wanted to relax after a full day, a day spent mostly on Lake Superior in a canoe. I felt the need to sink into that mental daze that comes with staring into a campfire. I'd picked up some driftwood while fishing. The wood had dried in the sun all day and was so dry it practically burst into flame when I set a match to the kindling. A couple of minutes later I was warming my backside from its heat.

I'd been privilege to a myriad of sensations all day. Unaccustomed to being so sensitive, the urge for downtime was almost overwhelming. It's a bit of a strange analogy, but the overload of sensory input that comes from living outdoors is similar to listening to your favorite rock band play a packed arena. You never want the music to end. But you realize as you leave, ears ringing, you need some quiet to recover in. Nightfall felt like a stage curtain being lowered, regrettable, but necessary.

By the end of September, nights are almost twelve hours long, a fact that can easily be overlooked when planning a camping trip to Isle Royale. It's not that anybody forgets their sleeping bag or tent, but little thought is given to what to do after dark. Tired or not, I can't sleep for twelve hours, not even ten hours, and falling asleep too early is something to avoid. When I did fall asleep early, I'd often wake in the middle of the night and lie there for hours waiting for dawn to arrive. To avoid falling asleep early, I waited until it was completely dark before making dinner. After dinner, I'd repair gear if need be, update the journal or try to read. But it isn't easy staying awake to read. I'd feel myself drifting off and have to stand up and walk around to wake up. Dinner, chores, journaling and some reading would maybe fill two hours of my evenings, which left another hour or two to try and stay awake in.

At home, inside a well-lit house, evenings are spent talking with family, watching TV, writing or reading, or even mowing the lawn or shoveling snow, maybe visiting friends. But on Isle Royale, in September, there aren't evenings as I normally think of them. There's not enough light. If it's overcast at night, it's difficult to see at all. It's not so dark that you can't see your hand wave in front of your face, but without a flashlight, you shouldn't stray far from camp for fear of walking into a low-hanging limb or trip on an unseen root.

The moon helps. It actually provides quite a bit of light, and once your eyes grow accustomed to the black shadows it casts, is surprisingly bright. The wildlife on Isle Royale also enjoys moonlit nights. Wolves do appear to howl at the moon. There is definitely more loon song and moose traffic. Whenever the moon was full, I wanted to howl, too … and did. (I doubt the wolves were fooled.) I came to eagerly await the moon's rising, and the sky felt empty when she waned. Moonless nights were a bit of a struggle.

The trouble is stars shed so little light. They do, however, make the sky appear bright by comparison. On moonless, clear nights, the sky is packed with starry flecks, light dusts and beacons. The stars fill the equivalent of an overhead bowl, and fill that bowl right down to its brim. On moonless nights, the stars became my silent camp-mates.

The sabbatical had begun over Labor Day Weekend, and for the first half of September the park was almost what I'd call busy. The shelters were filled with campers. You'd see several backpackers on the trails each day. Kayakers would come and go. During daylight hours, everyone was adventuring and not terribly social. But after dark, people gathered around each other's campfires, me included. When camping with friends and family, to stand around a fire at night is a wonderful time to relive the day's events, to tell stories or to talk deep into the night about your dreams and hopes and … troubles. You find your second-wind. I would see bobbing flashlights traversing the paths between each camp site as people visited one another. There's a real tribal feel to a campground after dark. You hear laughter break out, the thud of wood added to fires. Many campers stay up half the night. The accents of the Minnesotans versus the Wisconsin-ites or Michiganders, who are the park's primary visitors, drift across the campground. Once in a great while, you hear accents from more distant locales.

During the last two weeks of September, however, the campgrounds are typically empty and I had to find something else to do to fill my time after dark.

Shooting stars and Northern Lights are celestial events worth staying up for. They're Isle Royale's nighttime silent-film entertainment. There were nights when I'd stare skyward for so long that I began to feel like I was having a staring contest with the Almighty. Who was going to blink first? When He did, did He emit a flash of light? Shooting stars are often no more than a flash at the edge of sight. You wonder if you really saw one. By the time I turned my head to see it, I wondered if I really saw a shooting star or was that a trick of the eye?

Unlike shooting stars, Northern Lights begin subtly. If I'm going to be serious about waiting for a Northern Lights show, I needed to brace myself for a possible long vigil. They don't appear every night and sometimes not until the middle of the night. The Northern Lights (or Aurora Borealis—named after the Greek gods of dawn and the north wind) first appear as if it's a distant city's glow. As the glow slowly brightens, a single pale shaft of light timidly stretches south, appearing to climb the sky. The trembling patch or shaft looks as if it's testing the water. It moves forward and then retreats north, tries again, and retreats. Once satisfied, another swath of light joins in. The streaks begin to stretch farther south, and then another, until I know. This is no trick of the imagination.

If I'm lucky, the lights will gather overhead for a great dance, glowing with an incandescence that nearly blocks out the stars. Gleams shimmer and pulsate, quickly fading in and out, sometimes snapping into focus. There is no sound. Both transparent and visible, the lights tremble like ghosts.

Pale lights will splash the sky in hues of silver, greens, reds, violets, and white. They shift. They shake here, flash there. Some pulsate like coursing blood vessels. Others glow steadfastly, neither shimmering nor pulsating.

I can hardly look away, even when my neck hurt. If the pain reaches a point where I must change position, I sometimes would lie on the ground for a more comfortable view. But I've found that I can't lie down for long, and not due to the cold that seeps through my clothes, but because I became dizzy. Lying on the earth, my entire body in full contact with a spinning, revolving planet, I became woozy, almost sea sick.

A Northern Lights event is the ultimate little boy reward for staying up late. There were some nights when the stars would appear to be drawing closer to me—too close in fact. Things got a little too intimate. I felt like they might suck me into the cosmos. Are they trying to scatter my atoms into oblivion? At that point, I jumped up, planted my feet, and laughed.

There are far more stars than I can absorb with my narrow field of vision. I remember wishing I had eyes on the sides of my head for wide-angle vision, like birds or fish do. I wanted to view the entire sky without constantly turning my head. I also found I wasn't able to focus on a single star for more than a couple of minutes. It made my eyes water. I had to look away, and when I did, the star field sprang back into view, the one star lost as a blade of grass in a field.

The unthinkable number of stars overhead and their vividness give the distinct impression you're standing on the edge of an aerial sea. If I could just invert my existence and canoe those waters, what fish might I catch?

At times, I could see outlines of all manner of creatures and gods and battles. Like my forefathers, I occasionally slipped into an astrological outlook. Can you imagine what it would be like if I was there in January, when nights are sixteen hours long? What, then, would I begin to see?

Some nights I pretended to be a schoolchild again. How do I calculate the distance to that star or that one? If I left now, how long would it take to canoe to Orion's Belt? What direction would I take for our two courses to eventually converge? The star field is vast and beautiful and everything the poets say it is, but, as is my habit, I slip into science-mode. The light from Alpha Centauri, the closest star after the sun, takes 4.3 years to reach Earth. Its light travels at 186,000 miles per second. That means 4.3 years of light travel is the equivalent of 26 trillion miles. I scratched out the math in the sand.

From where I stood, I could see stars many times farther away than Alpha Centauri. I'd read that astronomers estimate that with the naked eye, a person standing at sea level can see stars as distant as 200 to 400 light years away. They calculate the distance to the nearer stars by creating giant triangles that are light years long. Using the diameter of the earth's orbit as the base of the triangle, they measure the tiny change in the angle of starlight made at opposite sides of the earth's orbit. The math may be simple geometry, but in a sense it is a problem that takes six months to solve. It took me awhile to recall the word astronomers use to label the process. The word is "parallax."

For stars more than 400 light years away, the distance is too great for the angle of light to shift enough to be detected, even by the most sensitive of instruments. The distance to those stars is measured by setting a star's light to a spectrograph. By taking measurements at different times of the year and from different places on the globe, the shifts in a star's signature pattern becomes large enough for astronomers to extrapolate the great distances involved. The astronomers admit it's a rudimentary method for making mega-light-year measurements, but accurate enough for estimates.

If I could look through the Hubbell Telescope, unencumbered by any atmosphere, I'd see stars and galaxies so distant that many scientists wonder if they are witnessing the beginnings of the universe. Even at light speed, it would take 13.7 billion years for the most distant star's light to make the journey to earth.

When I returned home, I'd read that the Hubbell telescope contributed to a multi-telescope sky survey called GOODS, or Great Observatories Origins Deep Survey. The combined telescopes focused on one direction in space for 90 hours, which doesn't seem that long, until you've tried to stare at a single star for five minutes. But to aim all of those telescopes in the same direction for 90 hours actually took researchers over a year to accomplish. The reason is every celestial body from meteors to planets to galaxies spins on its axis, and revolves around a planet or star, and are all traveling through space. They do so at incredible speeds. Taking only the Earth's spin into account, scientists calculate that if I was standing at the equator, I'd be traveling 1,024 miles per hour. The earth orbits the sun at a speed of 18.5 miles per second. Our solar system orbits within the Milky Way at a speed of 155 miles per second. The Milky Way travels through space in relation to nearby galaxies at a speed of another 185 miles per second.

My mind reels at the speed, but once in science mode and being late at night, it's hard to stop. I remembered that the Sloan Digital Sky Survey showed over one million galaxies in its efforts to create a three-dimensional map of one small section of sky. Even more amazing, the Sloan Digital Sky Survey and NASA's Wilkinson Microwave Anistropy Probe revealed a picture of a universe that appears to be expanding and expanding at an accelerating speed. "It is weird," Don Kennedy, editor-in-chief of *Science Magazine*, said in an interview with *USA Today*. "But there is widespread agreement that there isn't any other way to explain our universe."

Why galaxies are speeding away is a matter of scientific debate. Some astrophysicists believe space can be compared to a fabric with its edges being stretched, and as a result, the most distant galaxies are being pulled away from each other farther and faster. Other astrophysicists believe that as a direct result of the Big Bang, galaxies are moving away at an increasing rate of speed due to less gravitational pull from each other. Some believe the cause is a "dark-force," a term used to describe a theoretical anti-gravity power. For me that theory felt like a confirmation for worrying that the cosmos might suck my atoms into space.

It was definitely time for bed. The driftwood had burned down to fading embers, its red coals turning into charcoal grey. And it was too late to add more wood. I'm starting to grow cold. Closing my eyes, I listened for loon song and heard none. Do loons sleep?

The winds had calmed and the harbor had grown quiet. Even the ever-present rumble of surf from Lake Superior was stilled. I slowly stood, stretched my back and yawned. As I did, I dared to glance skyward one last time.

A shooting star flashed across the sky. It was a good one. The streak traveled from one horizon to the other.

Did He just say thank you for noticing?

Snuggling into the sleeping bag's down folds, I allowed the dark to swallow up infinity. I prayed for my family, and made a mental list of chores for tomorrow, then drifted off to sleep. Tomorrow should be another full day.

THE SCENT OF SPRUCE

"The farther one gets into the wilderness, the greater is the attraction of its lonely freedom."

~Theodore Roosevelt

THE MORNING IS FRESH AND DAMP. BIRDS WAKE AND PEEP SHYLY AT THE GROWING light. Every sound that finds its way into the Adirondack shelter where I wake reminds me of more familiar objects, certainly more familiar than distant galaxies or black holes. They are objects I can touch.

The shelters where mornings begin are the equivalent of a one-room, lean-to. They have a wooden floor and a shingled wooden roof. Three walls are made of two-by-six, tongue-and-groove planks with no windows. The front wall of the shelter is a screen that runs from the floor to the ceiling. A screen door opens onto a campsite in Chippewa Harbor that contains a picnic table and an outdoor grill. The grill is set atop a three-foot post. Not all of the campsites contain grills or fire rings. It depends on whether the Park Service allows wood fires at that particular campground.

Life on the island wakes slowly. The insects are sluggish, birds are less energetic, and the winds are generally calmer. Still groggy from staying up too late, I move slower, too. I unzip my bag, climb out and shuffle down the path to the beach to refill the coffee pot with water. I wade in knee-deep to go beyond the roiled water right next to shore. The chill is shocking. Standing in Lake Superior will bring you fully awake. I pump the water-filter handle and an agonizingly slow stream of filtered lake water fills the coffee pot.

When alone on mornings like these, and after coffee, I investigate unusual sounds or examine a plant not noticed before. I see the rabbits prefer chickweed as opposed to wood sorrel, that the fir trees have been browsed to eight feet high by the moose. Somewhere nearby, there's a wild rose in bloom. When first waking, my mind's eye notices objects I've passed by a hundred times before but only now register. The same is true for sounds. I try to locate that ubiquitous rustle, squeak, or splash that I hear a hundred times each day but now wonder about. There's a certain kind of joy in indulging these early morning curiosities.

Mist rises from the lake and the land is covered in dew. The scent of damp conifers is everywhere. Spruce and fir are the predominant trees of Isle Royale. They provide a green panorama year round, which is a welcome relief from the starkness of a land covered in snow and ice for a third of the year, and where the deciduous trees only hold leaves for five months. The clean winds blowing across Lake Superior through the millions of conifers make breathing alone worth the effort to reach Isle Royale. The air is so noteworthy that at one time an old highway sign posted near the departure point to the island, boasted, "You are now breathing the purest most vitalizing air on earth."

Treebeard the Ent, from J.R.R. Tolkien's, *The Lord of the Rings*, may best describe the experience. Treebeard is an ancient tree shepherd. Fangorn Forest is his domain, and he makes this remark about the air at the dawn of time:

"Those were the broad days! Time was when I could walk and sing all day and hear no more than the echo of my own voice in the hollow hills. The woods were like the woods of Lothlorien, only thicker, stronger, younger. And the smell of the air! I used to spend a week just breathing."

There are rare moments back home, when a breeze brings a scent of that same sort of clean air. The vitality on the wind makes me want to drop what I'm doing and seek its source like an animal on the hunt.

The air over Isle Royale smells fresh for good reason. The island's isolation amidst the largest freshwater lake in the world helps buffer the park from dust, pollutants and the other particulates that drift in the winds back on the mainland. The island has the unique distinction of doubling as a wilderness park for outdoor enthusiasts and being one of the world's foremost outdoor laboratories. For the ecologists, the water and air at Isle Royale has become the control subject for water and air quality testing. As mentioned, any contaminants found in the inland lake samples or by the air-monitoring equipment atop the Greenstone Ridge give scientists a reliable baseline for what is in the prevailing winds across the upper Midwest.

To breathe the air would be reason enough to spend a month on Isle Royale, but I'd hoped to do a little more than that. I'd wanted time to look around, to notice things. I'd hoped to pay attention to all of those little things that I felt were probably important, but weren't sure exactly how. I was hoping to pause long enough to find an answer to – What exactly is that?

I would stand outside the shelter at daybreak, drink my coffee, and follow a scent on the wind. I'd follow it until I located its source. If a strange stone caught my eye, I'd pocket it for further examination. Hearing squirrels chattering, I'd try to locate them in a forest of trees.

As it turns out, making time to pay attention to the little stuff proved to be more than just an opportunity to satisfy my curiosity. It was while studying the small and all of those seemingly inconsequential matters that I realized the small stuff makes all the difference to the big stuff. Having to rely on my equipment made that abundantly clear. If my fishing reel broke down, I didn't eat. If the flashlight batteries died, I can't see. If the tiny fuel jets in the camp stove clogged, if I lost my glasses, broke a paddle, the canoe springs a leak, or a great number of so-called little things went wrong, I was in big trouble. Living on a wilderness island for any length of time requires attention to the details, not to mention doing maintenance.

One morning, it was the adelgids that caught my attention. I see evidence of them all around the island. They're an unassuming little insect, and the spruce trees are infested with them. In fact, the damage they cause is so pervasive that it appears natural and, as a result, goes unnoticed. The insect itself looks like an aphid. They are pale green and somewhat pear shaped, but you rarely see the adelgids themselves. Their small size and color camouflage them, plus they expose themselves only for a few brief weeks during mid-summer. Only then can they be found on fir needles extracting fluids via their stylet-like mouthpart. The rest of the year they are hidden from sight, living inside spruce twigs. One would barely know they exist at all if they didn't damage the trees for what can be seen at any time of the year are the deformations they cause. They leave what can only be described as lumps on the twigs and branches.

These abnormal lumps, or growths of plant tissues, are called galls. Galls can form anywhere on a plant—on the trunk, in the branches, along twigs, roots, or on the petioles or leaves. Plant pathologists have identified several thousand kinds of galls, and they have been compared to tumors within the human body. Some galls are benign, others are malignant.

The galls caused by spruce adelgids are mostly benign, amounting to nothing more than nurseries for their young. Adelgids use the spruce twigs as brood hosts. A female adelgid flies from the fir tree, where she was feeding, to a spruce where she deposits 200 to 400 eggs inside a twig. Each egg is nestled inside an individual wood cell. The twig reacts to this intrusion by swelling around the eggs. The mass is green at first, but will fade to brown. Inside this protective covering the nymphs develop until they are ready to emerge. Once they emerge from their egg, (insects don't "hatch," they "emerge"), the nymph remains inside its wood cell and, for a brief time, feeds on the wood. When ready to depart, they chew their way free, and most of them fly to a nearby fir tree. A few will remain on the spruce.

Spruce adelgids are a relatively minor pest compared to gypsy moth caterpillars or the emerald ash borer. The adelgids cause mostly cosmetic damage and do little real harm to the tree. The lumps restrict sap flow, but not much. There are several different types of spruce adelgids, just like there are many different kinds of aphids. The spruce adelgids are so prolific and the brown lumps so numerous in the island's spruce trees that most people mistake the galls for branch nodes or cones.

There is no chemical or pesticide treatment to remove the galls once they form, and cutting out the numerous growths is a tedious task that can leave a tree looking mauled. The infestation, however, can be prevented from getting worse. A well-timed, single spray with the proper insecticide kills the newly emerging nymphs when they are at their most vulnerable stage. When the insects are eliminated, they stop creating new galls. The tree will eventually cover the lumps over with new growth, hiding them from view. It only takes about three years before there's enough new growth to sufficiently hide the galls.

I had to learn a great deal about this insect because it detracts from the appearance of valuable landscape trees. It's one of the more common pest problems I am asked to resolve. By becoming familiar with the adelgid's lifecycle, I became more effective at targeting and timing my pesticide applications. Before arborists understood its lifecycle, not to mention better understood the danger of the overuse of pesticides, we sprayed four or five times a year in hopes of catching the nymph when it was actively feeding. Sixty years ago, in fact, my predecessors used multiple applications of DDT.

I appreciate what our trade's learned about adelgids, and having a little time while on Isle Royale to think about them, I can't help but ask a few questions.

Why don't they feed and reproduce in the same genus? It would certainly be more efficient, not to mention convenient. Despite the name, "spruce adelgids" primarily feed on fir trees. They look similar, but spruce (*Picea*) and fir (*Abies*) are two completely different genera. Botanically speaking, the two are as different as a maple is from an oak or a willow from walnut. Travelling from a spruce to a fir and back again is risky business in the natural world. When the insect leaves its camouflage protection, it exposes itself to a host of birds and predators that feed on the delicate aphid-like nymphs.

There are nymphs called progrediens that recycle themselves. They never return to the spruce trees to reproduce. They keep feeding on the fir and morph into larger and larger nymphs until they just die off, never procreating. A different version sprouts wings, flies back to the spruce and lays eggs. There are nymphs that never leave the spruce tree and strictly feed at the base of the twig terminals.

Some female adelgids (parthenocarpic) actually emerge already impregnated, no mating necessary—an interesting concept with sobering implications for the males. Other types of female adelgids need to mate in order to reproduce.

Perhaps the most relevant mystery concerning this innocuous little bug relates to the galls they create. These insects are tiny to begin with, no larger than the capital A on this page. The small dab of adelgid fluid they apply to the twig is smaller yet. Yet this minute amount of fluid causes a severe reaction in the twig. The fluid is extremely potent. Studies are being done to see if any relationship exists between gall formations in plants and tumors in humans. By determining the chemical make-up of an insect's secretion, and how it induces plant malformations, researchers hope to learn what causes tumors, better understand allergic reactions and maybe even find a cure for some cancers.

Had I not studied spruce adelgids, I doubt I'd have noticed all of these brown lumps in the spruce trees. Yet, despite my education, I feel no closer to understanding them. It causes me to wonder what else I'm missing, and wonder what other people think about when they come to Isle Royale. Does a backpacking engineer marvel at how waves tumble and wish he could learn how to harness the energy? Does he think about designing a perpetual motion machine?

As she pulls her kayak onto shore, does the geologist see a pebble on the beach and wonder at the surf's rock-tumbler effect? Does she ask how old the stone is? Does the accountant stare at the stars like I do but, instead of asking how far away they are, question how to count them?

My early-morning explorations remind me of Mrs. Gerard, my third grade teacher. She tried so hard to make sense of the world for us. At eight-years-old, we asked simple, straightforward questions and naively expected straightforward answers in return. "Mrs. Gerard, what's stuff made from?" "How do fish breathe?" "Why did my cat die?"

She avoided the cat question, but did attempt to explain what stuff is made of. She gave us Tinker Toys to build scale models of molecules. Each student was given enough parts to attach two small wooden wheels of hydrogen atoms to a larger wheel of oxygen. Making it a group project, Mrs. Gerard had us progress to building some of the more complex sugars. We were told atoms and molecules are too small to see, but real, nonetheless. At eight, I remember thinking what a great teacher she was. Who else gives little boys toys to learn with? And I quickly forgot about building sugar molecules and started to build dinosaurs, not an easy object to build with Tinker Toys. I thought I was being creative. Mrs. Gerard didn't agree.

In fourth grade, Mrs. Powers said atoms are made from even smaller particles called electrons, protons and neutrons. These bits of electro-magnetized particles mimic planets orbiting the sun. The protons within the nucleus are so small, it would take 500 billion of them to fit in the dot on the letter i. She said everything from my baseball mitt to my teacher's freckles could be broken down into these charged particles.

I wondered when she would tell us, "That's it. There's nothing smaller. That's what we're made of."

As it turns out, we weren't even close. There are a number of smaller units—gluons, muons, and quarks for example. And scientists aren't even sure if they are particles or sparks of energy or both. Some say they are neither.

A recent theory gaining support among quantum physicists is Superstring Theory. It postulates that quarks, far smaller than electrons, could be made of infinitely smaller units. These units are postulated to be wiggling strings, loops or wavering bands of matter and energy. According to Brian Greene's book *The Elegant Universe*, superstrings are reported to be "about a hundred billion, billion times smaller than an atomic nucleus." These superstrings vibrate and bend at different frequencies, amplitudes and wavelengths. As best as I can understand it, the vibration frequency, amount of wavering, size of the strings, and tensile strength for each, make up the basic characteristics of matter and time. These superstrings can be roughly compared to strings on a piano or violin. The nature of the string and its resonance determine the character of each quark, which, in turn, eventually distinguishes an adelgid from a lake trout.

I liked superstring theory. Given the wonders I see, I wouldn't be surprised at all if music best describes the nature of all things.

If Ken were here listening to me search for the "essence of the universe," he'd tell me to lighten up and say we should be fishing. Ken captains a walleye charter boat on Saginaw Bay in Lake Huron and never seems to tire of the sport. Our first Isle Royale trips together entailed backpacking, though quickly evolved into canoeing so as to fish the island's world-class waters. He will join me for my last week of the sabbatical, and I look forward to the company, particularly his, as he well-understands the wonder of this island.

Beneath the stone I picked up earlier was a red worm. It quickly wriggled away under a fallen leaf. Ken would have wanted me to capture it for bait. I'd have told him the worm doesn't belong here. The reason I know this is that my son, Sam, informed me of the fact. He has friends who spent summers on the island studying earthworms. They are graduate students at Michigan Tech, and they did earthworm counts to determine the speed at which worms become established in a northern forest. Sam told me his friends would creep on their bellies across a designated quadrant of ground to count burrows and worms as they went. He said it had something to do with how earthworms change forest habitats. I asked him to explain, but he didn't know any more about it.

I found out later that earthworms are not native to Isle Royale or to most northern forests. Night crawlers aren't even native to the U.S. They are from Europe and have been spread, as one might suspect, by anglers. Prior to the National Park Service banning live or cut-bait on Isle Royale, worms likely went with fishermen to almost every inland lake.

When Sam first mentioned the earthworm study, it struck me as a big, "So what?" I think I even asked him, "Why are we spending research money on this?"

But while reading *The Earth Moved, the Remarkable Achievements of Earthworms* by Amy Stewart, I discovered that earthworms are voracious feeders, which is a difficult image to picture. But as I was to learn, earthworms turn over the soil as thoroughly as any farmer's plow. Earthworms feed on the organic matter that carpets the forest floor and, as they feed, vacuum off the leaf litter in the process. What they leave behind is a changed soil texture and altered bio-mass content.

Night crawlers, (*Lumbricus terrestris*) are much larger than their American cousins, two-to-three times larger, and are the alpha earthworms of North America. Night crawlers can quickly—surprisingly—turn a forest floor into the same muck I find in the tub of worms I buy at the bait store. When night crawlers remove the native micro-organisms from the soil, the entire forest habitat is affected from the ground up. The maple/beech forests, oak-woods or pine forests of the upper Midwest rely on native microbes to break down maple leaves, downed oak limbs or pine needles into the nutrients that maples, oaks, or pines prefer. The "good" microbes flavor the soil to the particular tastes that native trees prefer. And ... it's more than a matter of taste. If those good fungi and bacteria are eliminated, the trees are less able to intake important minerals. Trees can become weakened and stressed, making them more susceptible to droughts, insect attacks or diseases.

As advertised, earthworms are beneficial for flower and vegetable gardens and urban landscapes—no doubt a big reason night crawlers were brought here from Europe. But a northern forest needs different soil management than a garden does. In the north, the bio-material decomposes far more slowly than in warmer regions. When the glaciers receded, only 10,000 to 15,000 years ago at Isle Royale, there were no earthworms here. Transplanting earthworms, let alone night crawlers, into the north was like sending commercial trawlers into a pond.

Minnesota, Wisconsin and Michigan are packed with anglers who dream all week long about escaping come Saturday to their secret fishing hole. When they make their escape, worms often go with them. In the upper Midwest, it's difficult to find a location where night crawlers aren't present. In many places, the topsoil has become a microbial monoculture—focused exclusively around the lowly night crawler.

Fortunately, most of Isle Royale is free of earthworms, and no effort will be made to remove what's here. Besides being extremely expensive, the process of eliminating them would cause extensive damage to the already thin topsoil.

I shouldn't be surprised that foresters are studying earthworms. All of nature is inter-connected. When one item in the food-chain is altered, no matter how seemingly insignificant, there's always a cascade effect, and nowhere is that more evident than at Isle Royale where the island's mostly undisturbed setting is the perfect place for scientists to study that ripple effect. Scientists, as with any other professional, bring their own personal biases with them to the island. I had wondered what the engineers and accountants might see when they visit Isle Royale. It also makes me wonder what the other foresters notice. Foresters, like the trees they study, have branched a thousand different ways. Many perform services that are far different than what I do.

Scott Robinson is a perfect example. Our paths crossed on a golf course in St. Joseph, Michigan, some six hundred miles from Isle Royale. Scott works for ArborCom out of Toronto, Ontario, and he measures shade. He can tell me how much shade a tree casts on any given day of the year, at any hour of the day, for any tree species in the Midwest. He uses global positioning devices and a software program with CAD mapping to pinpoint shade density. He told me the 90-foot American elm at the dogleg on the 14th fairway at Point O Woods Country Club reduces sunlight by 31.9 percent on August 15th. A fairway that needs 80 percent sunshine to remain thick and healthy is important information for a high-profile golf course like Point O Woods where, as amateurs, Jack Nicholas and Tiger Woods played the Regional Pro-Am Tournament. Scott's shade study was so important to the members at Point O Woods (it's called Point O Woods for a reason) that the club spent six figures to acquire the shade data to justify to its members the need to remove a few trees.

Trees and turf are in constant competition for sunlight. Understandably, golf superintendents, whose responsibility it is to care for the turf, battle for their grass. They want to provide their greens and fairways with as much sunlight as possible. Grasses prefer full sun. Unfortunately for superintendents, country club members tend to love their trees. I once had a golf superintendent ask me if I would remove some trees in the middle of the night so he could avoid a confrontation. To the midnight raid, I said, "No."

If arborists won't protect trees, who will?

In the spring of 2002, a storm blew down more than two hundred trees at Point O Woods. No tornados were spotted but winds were clocked at over 90 mph. The superintendent, Ron Fox, told me that several golfers barely made it off the course in time. The storm was so severe it closed the club for two weeks in May, their peak season. Our tree service was hired to clean up the downed trees so they could reopen by Memorial Weekend.

Our entire company, forty employees strong at the time, showed up at the course the next morning, and with every piece of equipment we owned. It was while cleaning up the storm damage that I found Ron and his assistant, Jason, studying the grass on a newly seeded green. Ron had lent me a golf cart to coordinate the cleanup work. I needed to ask him the best way to move some trucks to another fairway without damaging their precious turf—an offense that will immediately get a tree service fired. When I rolled up to them in my cart, I found Ron and Jason on their hands and knees staring intently at a 12" x 12" section of a green. Their noses were no more than six inches from the ground.

I walked over, leaned down next to them and peered at the ground, forgetting my question and feeling like the person who sees someone on the street staring upward and joins a growing throng gazing into an empty sky.

Unable to see what the fascination was, I asked, "Did you lose a ring?" They turned their heads in unison, looked at me as if I wasn't there, and then turned back to study the green. Ron began to slowly stroke the turf with the palm of his hand as if he was checking the quality of an expensive fur.

Not able to contain myself—and on good terms with the both of them—asked again, "What the hell are you doing?"

Ron chuckled without looking up and said, "We reseeded this green a month ago, and are checking to see if it's ready for play. When you rub your palm against the grain, you know the green is thick enough when 100 blade tips stand on end per square foot."

"No way," I said.

"Bentgrass normally lies flat," Ron said. "That's why it works so well for greens. When you stroke the turf against the grain, it causes the blade tips to stand upright. We're counting blade tips."

They went back to their work, giving me no more notice. I left them staring at the ground. When I came back a half hour later, remembering my original question about how to safely move equipment, they'd moved a couple of feet over to check a different section of the green.

Some golf courses do spend a lot of money on their trees. They may buy lightning protection for them. Costs can range from $3,000 to $10,000 per tree. When a golf course is called Lone Pine Country Club, a lightning rod can save their irreplaceable landmark. Memorial trees, wedding trees and treaty trees may also warrant this expensive procedure.

A 250-year-old Southern live oak in Jacksonville, Florida, was recently installed with a lightning protection system. Legend has it that Native Americans and the Spanish signed peace treaties beneath its crown. The tree trunk is over 25 feet in circumference and the treetop rises to a height of 70 feet. Its crown spread is over 145 feet wide, with twisting branches that bow to the ground and curl back up. Florida arborists estimate the Treaty Oak could live another 400 years. It will continue to grow in girth if not in height as each year the tree lays on another ring of wood.

In 1986, the Jessie Ball duPont Foundation began a Jacksonville preservation program which grows seedlings from the Treaty Oak acorns. The Foundation makes them available for replanting throughout the city. Since the program was implemented, hundreds of seedlings have been planted, ensuring the legacy of the regal Jacksonville landmark.

Schools and parks also install lightning protection where the public congregates beneath a tree's canopy. Some species, such as cottonwoods, white pine and Norway spruce, are more prone to strikes than other species because they hold more water, making them better conductors. They may need to be removed if set on a knoll where people gather.

Installing lightning protection does not entail erecting a lightning rod, but connecting copper lines to the tree with insulated pins. The lines reach up to aerial points in the tree's crown. The points are placed well below the top since copper is a much better electrical conductor than a tree is. Lightning will bypass the treetop and travel down the lines to a ground-wire, which is buried 10 feet deep to safely discharge the blast. I am sometimes asked, "Won't the copper attract lightning?"

"I'm not sure," I say. "The manufacturer says it won't. I can tell you this much, no tree we've installed a system for has ever been damaged by lightning."

In the past 50 years, arboriculture has progressed from a person with clipboard and pencil in hand walking urban streets to assess parkway trees to - downloading aerial photos that can distinguish species, height, and overall health of every single tree. Arboriculture has evolved from tapping trees with rubber mallets to detect trunk decay to using Resist-o-graph machines that provide an EKG-like graph of the wood density. The trade has progressed from cleaning root collars with a hand trowel and a whisk broom to using supersonic air spades that jet the soil away. They miraculously leave the delicate hair-roots unharmed in the process, and an entire root system can now be exposed in a matter of minutes. We use drones to examine tree canopies.

Trying to understand how to use all of the new tools and stay atop the flood of information consumes much of my time. Deluged with data—much of it truly pertinent and helpful—I need to make sure I set time aside to actually go examine a real tree.

Clients are starting to email me digital photographs of their sick trees. My associates joke about the day when arborists will sit in front of a bank of monitors. We'll go online and view the tree from space, zooming in to see the sawfly caterpillar feeding on Mrs. Jones' red pine. Never leaving our chairs, we'll write a prescription and email it to the client, forwarding our prescription to the nearest Garden Center, where she can pick up her tree medicine. Maybe one day, we will be able to holograph our presence for a virtual one-on-one consultation. Courtesy of Facetime or Skype, we're almost there now.

The only problem is—I got into this business to work outdoors.

Times are changing, and changing swiftly. I've read that what keeps us sane is our brain's ability to filter all of the sensations that our bodies receive, utilizing only what's necessary. At Isle Royale, my senses grew far more acute, the load of input became overwhelming at times. I could easily see where a person could go crazy without a strong filter, and concluded that being a little numb wasn't always such a bad thing. By the end of the day, often weary to the bone, I was grateful my brain shut down each night as I slept.

I sit around a campfire and stare into a cosmos I'm told is expanding at a faster and faster rate of speed. In the morning, I scrutinize pebbles that are apparently made from infinitely tinier and tinier bits of matter and energy. I can't help but wonder about all those adelgids.

The world is a fascinating place and I am inherently curious about it. At birth, I began a lifelong journey of seeking answers to a million questions. I will ask questions until I can ask them no longer. Perhaps the biggest mystery is that no matter how much I learn or how skilled I become, the world does not grow any simpler. Instead, it grows increasingly more complex.

And, somehow, I'm all right with that.

DECISION MAKING TIME

"If a little knowledge is dangerous, where is the man who has so much as to be out of danger."

~Thomas Henry Huxley

THE ANNUAL CONFERENCE FOR THE AMERICAN SOCIETY OF CONSULTING ARBORISTS was being held in Palm Springs, California. Distance aside, Isle Royale is a long way from Palm Springs. Isle Royale is a wilderness island surrounded by the largest freshwater lake in the world. It sees well-over 200 inches of snow each winter, not to mention plenty of rain. Palm Springs, on the other hand, is a city that's surrounded by desert. The water…well…rain is mighty scarce.

The American Society of Arborists, (ASCA) is an organization I'm a proud member of, and, via their workshops, they've helped me to be a better expert witness, to mediate sensitive environmental dilemmas, write technical reports and more. The conference was being held at one of the many resorts that lie on the outskirts of Palm Springs, and despite the arid conditions, a lush green golf course surrounded the hotel. Plantings I rarely see; lemon trees, live oak, and eucalyptus thrived. The hibiscus was in full bloom and sage grew nearby given the scent that wafted through the open windows of the ballroom where I was there to listen to Dr. Glenn Haas speak.

Consistent with the organization's goal of making arborists better communicators, Dr. Glenn Haas, the keynote speaker, wasn't there to teach us about trees or habitat preservation or even lecture on how people interact with nature—his particular specialty. He was there, instead, to lecture on decision making. Back in October, while sitting at my desk in Michigan trying to decide whether the four-day conference was worth the expense, I had almost opted out. But the ASCA conferences are always held in December when my work tends to slow down, and they are always held somewhere scenic. It was while staring out a window at blowing snow, wrestling over whether or not to go that I decided a conference in Palm Springs sounded like a sensational idea. Settling into one of the ballroom chairs, I prepared to listen to Dr. Haas lecture me on how to make up my mind.

Dr. Haas is professor of Forest, Rangeland, and Watershed Management for the Warner College of Natural Resources at Colorado State University. His contributions to environmental stewardship are impressive. He is chairperson of the Federal Interagency Task Force on visitor capacity on public lands, and he co-chaired the International Symposium on Human Dimensions of Natural Resources in the Americas. His work and writings significantly influence how the two largest Federal land holding agencies, the National Park Service and the U.S. Forest Service, manage their lands.

When Dr. Haas took the podium, he thanked the moderator for his gracious introduction, and set his lecture notes on the dais. He picked up the remote for his Power Point presentation, flicked forward to be sure it was working, and then told us how grateful he was to be there, commenting on the beautiful surroundings. With that behind him, he then jumped right into his lecture.

"To put it bluntly," he began, "I'm here today because government officials are not making decisions. They're not just slow at it. They're not making decisions at all. And the problem is rampant.

"Unfortunately," he continued, "the research scientists are the worst of the lot. Given the task of deciding what measures to take about difficult land-use questions, the scientists continually want more time to complete their assignment. By the time they finally do make their recommendations, it's often too late. Either the issue had resolved itself or gone so far down a path there's no turning back. The feet-dragging has become so severe and so widespread, the U.S. Forest Service commissioned me to address the issue. They tasked me to resolve what might be called, 'The Procrastination Problem.'"

My attention started to waver. Slow decision-making by government officials, scientists wanting more time to do research—not exactly cutting-edge insights. But when Dr. Haas cited the controversial re-introduction of the timber wolf into Yellowstone National Park as an example, my interest piqued, for Isle Royale was in the throes of its own wolf controversy.

Dr. Haas recounted the well-known story of how the timber wolf was poisoned and trapped to near extinction in the U.S., and how the wolves have managed to make their way back to some of the more remote areas in the lower 48 states, primarily the upper Midwest and Northern Rockies. The partial recovery was boosted by a study that recommended that 66 wolves be imported from Canada and planted into the state of Idaho and into Yellowstone National Park.

Unlike Isle Royale, the wolves at Yellowstone can easily spread past the park's boundaries and soon did. Cattle and sheep were killed on nearby ranches. Elk and deer numbers tumbled. Even a few family pets disappeared. When you upset the ranchers and hunters, you've pretty much upset everybody who lives in the rural west. The wolves at Yellowstone soon created conflicts nobody had seen for a hundred years.

Dr. Haas told us that the same scientists who'd recommended introducing the wolves were given a new project: Write a management plan that somehow restrains an animal who's DNA compels it to free-range hunt.

While wildlife management officials studied the problem, land owners took matters into their own hands. Accustomed to dealing with problems themselves, which is hard not to do when the nearest authority may be a hundred miles away, ranchers were soon reverting to high-powered rifles and poison bait again. The whole matter gained national notoriety. It was, and still is, the quintessential endangered species dilemma. What is more important—protecting one's livelihood or protecting an endangered species?

According to Dr. Haas, the wildlife scientists kept stalling, asking their superiors for more time, saying it was a complicated issue, one that required a thorough investigation. As a result, environmental advocacy groups like The Nature Conservancy and the Sierra Club began to throw their considerable influence into the discussions, sending some of their best scientists (and attorneys) to the public hearings to speak on behalf of the wolves. The cattle associations, chambers of commerce, and business groups weighed in on behalf of their constituents. Mailings, TV spots and flyers went out. Convincing arguments were being made by both sides.

Dr. Haas said the arguments became increasingly heated, causing the wildlife scientists to grow all the more apprehensive. He said that when he caught up with them, he discovered that the real reason the scientists wanted more time to collect data and do surveys was that they felt no matter what they recommended, the whole matter was surely heading straight to court. The scientists wanted to secure iron-clad evidence to support their new plan. They didn't want to spend the next several years trying to convince everybody from the local magistrate up to the Supreme Court that they knew what they were talking about.

Isle Royale's wolf problem is the opposite of the Yellowstone dilemma. The question isn't what to do about a growing wolf population. It's what do we do about a shrinking one. As of the winter of 2015-16, only two wolves remain on the island. With only the two wolves to keep the moose in check, the moose population is booming. According to the recent winter study, approximately 1,250 moose live on an island that's only 48-miles long and 8-miles wide. That's more moose per square mile than anywhere else on earth. Without more wolves to cull the moose numbers, wildlife scientists predict that in three years the moose population will double.

The wolves were hunted out on Isle Royale prior to its becoming a National Park in 1931. Unlike Yellowstone, the wolves returned to Isle Royale naturally. Approximately 65 years ago, wolves crossed ice bridges that form between the island and Canada during colder winters. The moose, which are great swimmers, had arrived many years earlier by swimming there. When the wolves arrived, they found over 2,000 moose living on the island.

Those first few wolves must have felt like they'd stepped into a banquet hall. Courtesy of Lake Superior, the abundant moose population was penned inside the equivalent of a corral. Within a few short years, moose numbers crashed and for the next sixty years, the wolves and moose developed a precarious predator-prey balance. Without the moose, the wolves would starve. Moose are the only reliable food source during the long winters. And without the wolves to cull them, the moose would overrun the island and eliminate their winter food sources.

Normally, the solution to the current imbalance would be simple—introduce more wolves. There's no concern about wolves spreading onto ranches or hurting the hunting, which isn't allowed in the park. The hang-up is the wilderness status of Isle Royale National Park. It prevents the wildlife scientists from stepping in. They can monitor the wildlife. They are not allowed to interfere.

There are no deer, bear, elk or caribou on Isle Royale. There are also no smaller mammals such as raccoons, opossums, skunks, woodchucks or badgers. The distance from the mainland to the island (12-miles) is too great for the majority of the animals to swim, and the smaller mammals and bears hibernate during the winter when ice bridges form. While woodland caribou, lynx and coyotes once called Isle Royale home, they were hunted out prior to the establishment of the park and have not returned. The wolves and moose, not counting us humans, are now the only large mammals.

Wildlife scientists have called Isle Royale the perfect place to study such a singular mammalian predator - prey relationship. Viewable from the air during the winter, the moose and wolves are relatively easy to count. There are no leaves to screen the view. The snow-covered ground and ice-covered lakes also make a great backdrop to see large, dark-brown animals. Fly low enough, you can see tracks. The study is in its 57th continuous year, making it the longest ongoing predator - prey study in the world.

The Isle Royale wolf-moose study has played a major role in proving the value of large predators. Wolves help cull the weak and infirm from moose, elk, deer and caribou herds, leaving the strongest and most virile animals to procreate. Combined with the 1983 film rendition of Farley Mowat's book, *Never Cry Wolf*, the general public is now largely convinced that predators are an integral part of any ecosystem. When Mowat's book was published in 1963, it was a case that desperately needed made. The wolves had carried the Big Bad Wolf stigma far too long. Fifty years later, it is fairly common knowledge that wolves present little threat to humans. There are rare documented cases of wolves attacking people. None have ever occurred on Isle Royale.

Lake Superior is a big reason the Isle Royale wolves did so well—at first. The lake essentially penned-in the moose. But the lake, in a sense, is also the reason for the cause of the wolves' decline. Fewer and fewer ice bridges have been forming in recent years, which results in fewer and fewer new wolves making their way to the island to augment the island's wolf population. The last known wolf to migrate to Isle Royale and remain was in 1997. Known as "The Old Gray Guy," he helped bolster a gene pool that was already in decline. Only thirteen wolves remained in 1997 from a high of fifty in 1980. The Old Gray Guy quickly became an alpha male and wolf-counts briefly rose for the next ten years, but once again started to fall. With no new blood since then to infuse a healthy diversity of genes, the island's population of wolves began suffering from in-breeding problems. The excessive in-breeding has caused several genetic issues such as spinal malformation, reduced disease resistance and reduced reproductive rates.

In 2013, only nine wolves remained on the island and for the first time in the history of the predator–prey study, the island's science team recommended to the National Park Service that wolves be introduced. The Park Service has final authority in the matter. The recommendation by the scientists to introduce wolves wasn't a position they always held. The scientists had long supported the hands-off policy. They felt studying a strictly wild population made the island project especially relevant.

What changed their minds, according to lead scientists, Dr. Peterson and Dr. Vucetich, was when three wolves perished down an abandoned mine shaft in 2012. Apparently, a snow bridge over the mine opening collapsed beneath them. Since a mine shaft is not "natural," but human-caused, obviously man has already interfered with the island wolves whether we want to admit it or not. And with the evidence of global warming, researchers also claim that fewer ice bridges are forming, making it less possible for wolves to repopulate the island naturally. They support that evidence with satellite photography of Lake Superior that goes back several decades.

Still, the National Park Service is reluctant to change the 57-year hands-off policy. The policy is integral to more than just the wolf-moose study. They say it's also important to the other wildlife studies being done on the island, as well as across the nation. A change might set an unwanted precedent. An intervention could allow commercial concerns to legitimately ask why they, too, can't hold more influence.

In a reversal of roles, the general public, particularly the locals, are for introducing wolves. The wolves add a certain wilderness tension that attracts visitors to the park, which brings in much needed commerce to the rural communities that are the conduits for transportation to the island. Considerable public pressure is being brought to bear on the Park Service to introduce wolves.

Sounding all too familiar, the National Park Service says they need more time to study the issue. They want a wolf-moose vegetation management plan created and an environmental impact statement created first. The delay has received national attention. Articles have been written about the island's wolves in the New York Times. It's been covered by NPR and written about in several science-related magazines.

A spark of hope for a natural resolution appeared last winter, when two wolves were spotted crossing the ice from Canada heading for Isle Royale. The winter of 2014-2015 was an exceptionally cold one, and Lake Superior froze over between the western end of Isle Royale and the Grand Portage Indian Reservation in Canada. Spotters watched two wolves from the air and anxiously followed their progress. Both wolves safely reached the island. They followed the shoreline around the western end of the island to the far south side, eventually reaching Siskwit Bay.

Inexplicably, they returned to Canada five days later.

According to Dr. Peterson and Dr. Vucetich, it is unlikely the two wolves would have made any difference. They think it's too late now. The island needs more than just two wolves to restore a healthy population. Regardless, the wolves' departure was a disappointing setback.

Sadly for the island's last remaining wolves, which have never been named as far as I know, predictions are it will take the Park Service three years to complete their studies and another year to write a new plan. There's no question in anyone's minds that the delay means the demise of the island's last two wolves. Barring some miraculous migration of an entire pack or two, it is safe to say that within the next five years, wolves will no longer call Isle Royale home.

As for my own personal feelings on their dilemma, I must say I feel torn about it. I can appreciate the Park Services' position. Their researchers are well aware of how important it is to establish a healthy predator - prey balance. They fully understand that without wolves, too many moose will alter island habitats, and those changes will in turn affect the rest of the flora and fauna.

With that said, shouldn't there be at least one place on this planet where man never directly interferes with nature? With Isle Royale's laboratory-like isolated setting, the park is arguably a perfect place for that to happen.

*

Dr. Haas scanned his audience. His notes were so close to the microphone that when he turned a page, the paper's rustle could be heard at the back of the room.

"The Yellowstone scientists were stuck," he told us. And wanting more time made sense to them. They complained that performing good science takes time. You need to make sure the data is accurate, well-organized, relevant and complete. You need to be sure your conclusions are congruent with the data.

Dr. Haas asked us, "Can you not relate with them? As consulting arborists, you too are men and women of science. You collect data, hopefully being careful that it's accurate and relevant. You, too, are pressed to make fact-based recommendations. How do you reach a level of certainty that enables you to create sound, science-based decisions? Have you ever been less than certain about your diagnosis, your recommendations? Have you ever been asked to resolve tricky, intricate issues where you want more time to study the issue? Certainty can be a slippery objective, can it not?

"We strive for certainty—for proof," he added. "We normally achieve proofs by running experiment after experiment until we come up with the same results each time. But to achieve those consistent results, we need to eliminate so many variables that often our experiments barely resemble the real world. The Yellowstone team had to work in the real world: a world where all of the complicated variables need fair and balanced consideration, not elimination. And they were being pressured from all sides to 'Hurry up!'"

Pausing for effect, Dr. Haas asked his audience, "If people follow your advice, are you fearful of the consequences? Have you ever been afraid of being sued if things go wrong?"

A dozen such incidents sprang to my mind. Several heads nodded across the room. One of the big reasons I'd joined ASCA was to learn how to reduce my liability.

Dr. Haas waited for the room to quiet.

"As consultants, you don't get called in unless there's a problem, likely a controversial one. If the solutions were clear, they wouldn't call you. So then, how do we propose solutions to emotional, complicated issues when the 'preponderance of evidence,' as the attorneys like to call it, leaves us scratching our heads?"

If Dr. Haas hadn't had my full attention before, he certainly did now. He'd placed his finger on a matter that had bothered me for a long time, bothered me more than he knew.

There are countless instances where my tree care recommendations can't guarantee a tree will survive. I sometimes can't even guarantee my diagnosis is correct. The worst cases are the risk assessments. People want to know if their tree is safe. "Will my tree fall on my house, the playground, a child?" All trees eventually fall. People want to know when. They don't expect a day and hour. But they do want some reasonable time frame. Expert or not, I can't always tell.

In the summer, I'd been asked to assess six big oaks to be used as supports for a new zip-line course. Thousands of people would trust their lives to those trees. How much wind is too much? How much strain is too great? There are no hard and fast guidelines for those thresholds. Even the strongest of oaks can fail.

Mrs. VanPortfleit, a long-time customer, called again this fall to ask about her prized sycamore—the one that leans over her patio. An early ice storm had caused it to sag.

"Do you think it might break?" she asked me.

I remember thinking, how do I know how much weight the ice adds?

Last year, a family sued a campground when a big cottonwood—the one with the rope swing that kids use to drop into the river—unexpectedly fell and crushed an RV with a woman inside. She was seriously injured. The family sued the campground.

The attorney for the owners of the campground asked me to determine if the staff should have seen the catastrophe coming. "Mr. Foerster, is it reasonable to think they could have prevented the accident?"

The fallen cottonwood was completely removed by the time I got called-in. All that was left of the tree were old photographs and the stump. Their attorney said chances were good this one's going to court. Prepare yourself. You will be deposed. You will have to testify.

I couldn't help but ask how I was supposed to know what the campground staff should know about trees? I'm an arborist not a psychologist. And when there's no tree to examine any longer, how am I supposed to determine if the cottonwood presented a danger, obvious or otherwise?

Those were difficult cases. They caused me a great deal of nail-biting. And while I can say I know something about trees, what about those decisions I must make about issues I'm not an expert on? If experts struggle over matters we're knowledgeable about, how can a jury of your peers—plumbers, waitresses, accountants, and … arborists, all amateurs by comparison—decide a person's fate at trial?

Who wants to do jury duty? Who has time for it? I'd already asked the court to excuse me once, when the jury duty notice arrived in the spring, our busy season. The judge graciously allowed it, but only if I would serve in the fall.

The notice came in September, and I was instructed to arrive at the courthouse by 9:00 a.m., October 15th. When I arrived, there were a hundred other potential jurists milling about the assembly room, and nobody else looked too thrilled to be there either. At 9:30, a court reporter walked in and asked if everyone had signed in. She quickly separated us into three groups. Each group, she told us, would be sent to their respective courtrooms where jury selection would take place. Given the current case load, she said chances were less than fifty-fifty of being selected. To my dismay, sixty minutes later I was sitting in a jurors' box with 13 other citizens assigned to a trial.

They don't always tell you what the charges are during jury selection. They ask if you know the defendant or the plaintiff. They ask if you know the attorneys or the judge, and what you do for a living. The judge asks whether you hold any particular bias or grudge against a gender, race, or trade, particularly any bias against the law enforcement profession. But it wasn't until we were sitting in the jurors' box two weeks later, the courtroom filled with friends and family, and the trial set to begin that the judge told us why we were all there. When he did, a collective gasp went through the jurors' box. Several of us blanched and groaned.

It was a horrendous crime, a crime that need not be described here. The case was so sensational that the Chief Magistrate for the district court said he decided to preside over the trial himself.

After he read the charges to the packed courtroom, and seeing the juror's faces, he allowed us a moment to collect ourselves. He turned to the recorder, said something we couldn't hear, and organized some papers on the bench. A moment later, he cleared his throat and turned to face us.

He informed us that for this trial there would be no argument by either side about the cause of the injury. Both sides had agreed to the cause. He said this would strictly be a case of whether or not the defendant committed the crime. Is she guilty or not guilty?

I glanced at the woman next to me in the juror's box. She looked to be about thirty years old, well-dressed. She was breathing hard, and her face was chalk-white, like she might faint. She mumbled under her breath, "I don't think I can do this."

I didn't know what to tell her. Given the injuries inflicted, I wasn't sure I could either.

"Ladies and gentlemen of the jury please give me your full attention," the judge said with some authority. More softly, he continued, "Let me begin by saying thank you for being here today. Jurors are the backbone of this nation's judicial system. In my opinion, jury duty is equivalent to serving in the armed forces, and jury pay, as you well know, has never been commensurate with the service you provide or the sacrifices you make. This trial, I predict, will take up to a month-long. We will spend much of that time together, folks."

A few jurors groaned again.

Rocking forward in his leather upholstered, high-backed chair, the judge informed us that during the trial, and during the deliberations that would follow, we were not allowed to speak to anyone about the proceedings. If you accidently see TV coverage or hear radio updates, change the channel. "You will be tempted to talk about the trial to loved ones or friends. Don't!" he warned. "Evidence and testimony brought forward in the trial, and only that evidence and testimony you receive in this courtroom, should contribute to your decision."

If the press becomes a problem, he cautioned us, or the case gains too much attention, he said it may become necessary for him to sequester us.

"And let's all hope that isn't necessary."

No kidding, I thought.

He went on to explain that there would be no eye-witnesses testifying—or none that would admit to it. Our verdict would be based on circumstantial evidence and the opinions of expert witnesses. He said that both the prosecution and the defense were calling in several medical experts to testify. Some were flying in from New York and Chicago. These doctors would testify to the likelihood, or not, of the defendant's guilt or innocence. As jurors, he explained, you can either believe or disbelieve expert opinion. Equally important, he added, you can believe or disbelieve their opinion is relevant.

Along with expert witnesses, a great deal of circumstantial evidence would also be presented. To help us better understand what circumstantial evidence is, the judge explained that circumstantial evidence could best be described by the following analogy.

You wake up in the morning, pull your window curtains open, and look outdoors to find a fresh coat of snow on the ground. If you looked out that same window when you went to bed the night before and there was no snow on the ground, you may assume correctly it snowed sometime during the night. If you looked out your window and saw no tracks in the snow across your front lawn at eight in the morning and you then returned one hour later and saw tracks, you can be certain that someone walked across your front lawn between eight and nine o'clock. You may not know who that person is, but you can rest assured someone crossed your lawn between those hours. That's circumstantial evidence.

He finished his instructions with, "Before we commence with opening arguments, are there any questions?"

There were none.

And so began one of the most difficult months of my life, not to mention, at the end, making one of my life's most difficult decisions.

The defendant adamantly denied hurting the child. Neighbors of the defendant testified how she could never commit such an act. With tears flowing down the defendant's cheeks, she testified under oath that she simply did not do it.

She had two pre-school age children. If convicted, she would rarely see them again.

Both parents of the injured child testified, as well. Tears flowed down their faces, also. They both swore with equal fervor how the defendant did commit the crime.

The medical examiner from the hospital testified that it was his opinion the child was injured on the same day that he saw the child, which clearly implicated the defendant. The doctor told the jury he'd contacted the police that same night. He said that's standard practice for suspected abuse cases.

The police detectives who investigated the incident testified how they'd gone to the hospital that same night to talk to the medical examiner. They also talked with the parents. The next morning the detectives went to the defendant's home to question her. They had interviewed her for over two hours and an arrest was made one week later.

Both sides presented a blizzard of lab reports, police reports, and medical opinions.

The defendant must have come from a wealthy family for they retained one of the areas' most acclaimed defense attorneys. He had hired three separate medical doctors who were expert on symptoms related to the injuries. All three of the doctors disagreed with the examiner's opinion. They testified how it was medically impossible to pinpoint within a couple of day's time when a person has been injured in such a manner.

The defense attorney did everything in his power to implicate the parents for the crime, though no tangible evidence was ever brought forward.

The three weeks of testimonies was culminated by three more hours of closing arguments. When finished, the judge reminded us once again that our decision must be based strictly on the evidence presented at trial, and that we need to reach a unanimous decision.

He then dismissed us to the juror's room.

※

Dr. Haas took off his glasses, gently set them down, and stepped out from behind the podium. "Ladies and Gentlemen ... what you do is difficult." He stuck his hands in his trouser pockets and looked down for a second, and then slowly looked up. "Experts or not, you don't attend conferences like this one if you think you have it all figured out. Trees are complicated. They're multi-faceted, living, breathing beings. The habitats and environs where they grow are even more complicated. When broken into their parts—the soil, water, air, temperature, light, micro-biology, pests, predators, etc.—they all play off one another. Lord knows, the people we work for can be complicated, not to mention difficult. The relationship between people and trees is often an unclear one. I ought to know. Is it any wonder we want more time to do our jobs? Yet, decisions must be made ... and in a timely manner."

"Let me offer you a little advice. It's advice about reaching a decision, I received about four years ago, and from a most unusual source.

"Interestingly," he continued. "I didn't receive this counsel from a priest, nor from my saintly father, God rest his soul. I received this advice from a guy who can throw a shadow on any fact, who can cause you to doubt you're sitting in this ballroom. He is one of the most evasive people I know, definitely a guy who loves a good debate.

"He is an attorney. He also happens to be a good friend of mine.

"We were walking together to a local restaurant from the college campus where we both work. I was complaining to him about how the scientists assigned to land-use questions dread court. I told him they constantly drag their feet. They'll do almost anything to avoid litigation, including not completing their work. The delays are slowing much-needed actions. I informed him about the Yellowstone problem. The scientists keep asking me, 'How can I keep from being sued?'

"To my consternation, my friend laughed at me. "'Glen,' he said, 'you can't avoid court. For matters as sticky as the Yellowstone issue, there's no avoiding it. There's an old legal axiom that goes: You can be sued by anyone, at any time, and for any reason. The problem isn't how to avoid court. That's a foregone conclusion with matters as controversial as the Yellowstone situation. You just want to make sure you win.'"

"'What do you mean?'" I asked him.

"'Glen, tell your scientists that all they need to do is … their due diligence. Due diligence means, record all the data. Clearly demonstrate how you acquired the data. Show how it points to your conclusions.'"

"'That seems a bit simplistic,' I complained."

"'Glen, tell them to do their jobs. Right or wrong, once the court accepts them as experts, and they are experts, right?'"

"'Yes, they certainly are. They're some of the smartest, most well-educated people in the world.'"

"Right. Then, all they need to do is show the court how they came to their conclusions. The courts call an expert's conclusions "opinions" for a reason. They don't call them facts. They don't call them answers. They call an expert's testimony, "opinions." As long as their conclusions make sense, they'll be fine.'"

Armed with his friend's advice, Dr. Haas told us that he soon convinced the Yellowstone scientists to complete their new management plan.

They eventually recommended a policy change that allowed for a quicker permit process for dispatching problem wolves. They also recommended the no-wolf-hunting policy be continued. They strongly recommended adding staff to more closely monitor the situation.

Not surprisingly, Dr. Haas told us nobody was happy with the plan. The ranchers weren't happy, given the slow response in the past to their cries for help, yet they grudgingly accepted it. They recognized that the compromise finally allowed them a legal way to protect themselves.

The environmental groups were also far from happy. But given the no hunting stipulation, they, too, reluctantly agreed.

Everybody was finally able to move on.

Dr. Haas wrapped up his lecture with, "In conclusion, ladies and gentlemen, the Yellowstone recommendations aren't very scientific sounding, are they? The new plan sounds more like a treaty than a scientific study. If you were to read the recommendations, there is no summary section. There's no mention made of projected wolf counts or predictions of cattle losses. Yet they created what is in my opinion a real-world solution. In our business, that's often all we can hope for."

✳

The court bailiff led us single-file to the jurors' room, which was a corner office on the fifth floor of the courthouse. Since we were about to be locked inside, I was happy to see it had big windows overlooking the city in two directions. There was a long oval table in the middle of the room with enough chairs for each of us to sit. Once all fourteen jurors entered the room, the bailiff told us to knock if we needed anything. She said she would return every two hours to check on progress, and then closed and locked the door behind her.

After three long weeks of not being allowed to whisper a word about the trial to anyone, including each other, conversation erupted. Twelve jurors and two alternates all talked at once. The walls of the jurors' rooms are supposed to be soundproof. I doubt they were thick enough.

"Do you think her tears were real?"

"Did anyone else notice how the father looked like he couldn't breathe?"

"Do you remember Dr. Caldwell? I thought he seemed weird."

"The medical examiner wouldn't look us in the eye."

"Do you think the neighbor hesitated when she said she still trusted her?"

We all had questions. We each wanted to know how the other interpreted testimony. We vented for two full hours before someone finally said above the din, "Where are we at? Let's take a vote."

The jury foreman, Karen, asked for quiet.

When everyone settled down, she said, "That's a good idea. Raise your hand if you think she's guilty."

Seven people voted guilty.

"Raise your hand if you think she's not guilty."

Seven voted not guilty.

There was a long silence and conversation erupted again.

If the trial had been difficult, deliberations were worse. We wrestled over the verdict for five solid days. Everyone was civil, but the strain mounted as each day passed with no agreement.

We all lost weight. After one particularly intense day, I was so preoccupied with deciding a verdict that I drove straight through a stop sign on the way home from court. It was an intersection I'd stopped at for years. Fortunately, the only other person at the corner was a driver coming the opposite way. He blasted his horn as I cruised through the stop, my foot never touching the brake.

Each day, we took several votes. We never came closer than an eight-to-four spread.

Four of the jurors never wavered on their guilty verdict. Four other jurors never wavered on not guilty. Four of the jurors vacillated back and forth.

Even the two alternates, who are chosen by lot, were split.

After the third day of deliberations we knew we were in trouble. The foreman asked me to knock on the door and ask the bailiff if we could see the judge.

The judge allowed us to re-enter the courtroom—all in front of the attorneys and families and friends, who I'm sure were in anticipation of a verdict. We told the judge we were deadlocked.

The judge sent us back to the juror's room, telling us to keep trying.

He told us the same after the fourth day.

Three times that week we asked the judge for transcripts from portions of the trial. They were testimonies we wanted further clarification about. Juror's requests for trial transcripts are an almost unheard of request to be allowed. But hearing of our deadlock, the judge allowed it all three times.

At the end of the fifth day, the twelve of us filed back into the courtroom. The two alternates had been sent home.

The judge asked if we had reached a verdict.

Karen stood and informed the court we remained deadlocked. To be certain, the judge asked each one of us to stand in turn, and one at a time say aloud to the gallery whether we felt there was no hope of reaching a unanimous verdict. We were all sure. It was the only unanimous decision we made.

He declared a mistrial.

As he slammed down his gavel, the judge said we were only the second hung jury he'd seen in his 23-year career.

We returned to the jurors' room, and after saying our goodbyes and promising to stay in touch, I was moved by how close we'd all grown to one another, and in so short a time. Despite our rift down the middle, and despite some intense arguments, (at times, shouting at each other at the top of our lungs), I think we all understood how difficult the trial was for each and every one of us.

I lost ten pounds that month and felt like I'd aged ten years. For my part, I honestly couldn't tell who was telling the truth—the defendant or the child's parents. One side or the other was lying. To this day, I'm not sure which.

In the end, the doctors for the defense had convinced me there was no way to be certain when the injury occurred. And the judge's instructions to us were clear. *You must presume innocence unless there are no reasonable doubts as to the defendant's guilt.* I had reasonable doubts. I thought she probably committed the crime, but I couldn't convict her without clearer evidence. For me, the defendant's medical experts had wiped out the footprints in the snow.

I voted not guilty.

Eight months later, I ran into one of the jurors at the grocery store. We hugged and I asked her what was new in her life. She said she'd followed the retrial and told me the woman was convicted.

She said the one doctor for the defense, the one who'd convinced several of us that we couldn't be sure when the injury occurred, was snowed in at LaGuardia Airport during a three-day blizzard. The judge would not postpone despite the defense attorney's pleas.

A month later the defendant was sentenced. I never heard how long she was to be imprisoned.

✳

Sitting in that ballroom in Palm Springs listening to Dr. Haas lecture us about decision making, he caused me to wonder again about the fate of the defendant. And despite Dr. Haas' wise advice, not to mention that of a respected judge, I couldn't help but still feel like some decisions are too difficult to make.

Yet, decisions must be made.

It sounds so easy. Consider all of the evidence. Review the data's sources objectively. Give fair consideration to every side. Listen to the experts—keeping in mind their conclusions are only opinions. Weigh everything.

Then make a decision.

Easy to say, tough to do.

A few years later, I was sitting in a brewery with an attorney friend of my own. By chance, we began to discuss a judge's decision about a totally different case that involved parental custody of minor children.

He said, "I bet that didn't go well."

Surprised, I said, "No, it didn't. How did you know?"

He said, "The courts generally hand out what is called in the trade, 'rough justice.'"

I knew the parents involved. The ruling was indeed harsh and nobody walked out of the courtroom happy.

He gave me a grim smile. "People think that by going to court they're going to receive a fair hearing, receive "'justice,'" maybe receive some sort of Solomon-like decision. Nobody's that wise. Right or wrong, a judge is merely the person who has no choice but to render a decision.

Errors, Miscues, and Humiliations

" ... if we ever meet him, we'll know it, he will still be so angry."

~*Tecumseh* by Mary Oliver

SEEING DISGUST IN A GENTLE SOUL'S EYES, SENSING ONLY ANGER BROILING WITHIN them, and knowing that all of that loathing is directed at me is an experience I don't quickly forget. Mean-spirited people can scowl, and for the most part I shrug it off as being their normal demeanor. But when a person who normally has nothing but kind words to say, who views the world through rose-colored glasses, and has a perpetual sunny disposition looks at me as if I'm no better than a snake oil salesman. It's an encounter I lose sleep over.

Mrs. Tanner was doing her best to be polite. But I'd failed her. Her ancient elm was dying, and it was too late to do anything about it. I'd misdiagnosed the problem, thinking the die-back was the early onset of Dutch elm disease. I'd charged her a healthy fee for the ensuing treatments. From the look of their home and the clothes that she wore, not to mention the outfits of her four young children playing in the yard, I doubted the family had much disposable income to devote to tree care. She'd been patient. She'd called for a follow-up visit when the tree didn't improve after six months. I'd missed the problem again, explaining at the time the difficulty of stopping Dutch elm disease. When it became clear to her the next spring that the treatments failed, she consulted with another arborist, who correctly diagnosed the problem.

The elm had a basal canker. Cankers are a generic term for a wood tissue infection. This infection was at the base of the tree and treatable if identified early enough—before it spreads too far and girdles the tree, which had now occurred.

I stood in the middle of her front yard in June, the old elm dropping pale green and yellow leaves. She told me that she wished her husband could be there, but said he couldn't afford to take the time off from work. Waves of disappointment radiated from her. Yet even with the loss of her once graceful, iconic elm—one of the few remaining in the neighborhood—she never once swore at me or raised her voice. I wish she had.

By that time I'd been working in the tree business for fifteen years and was, I thought, entering my prime as an arborist. I'd seen many a tree-issue. But mistakes are easy to make in this trade. I'd become well-practiced at admitting when I'm wrong, and had grown mature enough to own up to my mistakes. I'd learned that dodging these painful confrontations tend to only make matters worse. I should have profusely apologized and recommended we remove the tree, perhaps at no charge.

Instead, given her obvious lack of confidence in me, I suggested, "Perhaps it would be best if I send another arborist from our company to resolve this for you?"

She quickly said, "Yes."

I never saw her again.

The tree service bailed me out. Another one of our arborists did meet with Mrs. Tanner, and did offer to remove the tree at no charge. Afterwards, Pete, the owner of our tree service, called me into his office to hear what happened. He decided not to hold the whole unfortunate incident against me, explaining that these mistakes sometimes happen. Dutch elm disease, he said, is a common problem for elms. Given the symptoms, 99 times out of 100 you'd have been correct. But the fact that we're busy in the spring, he said, is no excuse. You hurried your examination and you presumed it was just another case of Dutch elm disease.

"Next time, Vic, please be more careful."

One of my early mentors told me shortly after I started working at the tree service that generally only one or two pests cause 90 percent of a tree's problems. Bob Kelly had been working in the tree business for thirty years. He told me every tree species has its one or two nemesis. "If you know those one or two pests, and which tree they prefer, you'll become a good arborist." Emerald ash borers for ash trees, locust plantbugs for locusts, and willow leaf beetles for willows are pests so common to those species, the insects are named after them.

After pointing out to me how easy it was to become a so-called good arborist, Bob would then add with a twinkle in his Irish eyes, "An expert, however, is someone who can identify the other 10 percent of the problems. And that, my boy, takes a long time to learn. Oh, and by the way, people rarely call an arborist for the easy ones."

In Michigan it shouldn't be difficult to become what Bob calls a "good" arborist. There are typically only 10-to-12 different tree species found on any one acre of woods. Many times there's less. There may be hundreds of different species in an acre of rainforest, but as one travels north and the growing season shortens, that number of tree species dwindles to zero when the tundra is reached. It didn't take me long to learn the dozen common trees of Michigan and their one or two most common pests.

Similarly, the typical residential landscape normally contains only two or three of the twelve most commonly planted trees. The little diversity is due in part to Michigan's northern climate, but it is more often due to the public only planting trees they are familiar with, and nurseries, in business to make money, grow the trees customers ask for. It's somewhat of a Catch—22. The lack of diversity is one reason invasive species make such a big dent in tree populations. If a pest focuses on a species like ash or elm, we lose close to ten percent of all of the trees in the region.

Using their common names, the most planted trees in Southern Michigan are white pine (the State tree), Colorado spruce, eastern hemlock, red maple, sugar maple, London plane tree (sycamore), honey locust, linden, ornamental pear, flowering crab, hawthorn, river birch and Japanese maple. (Some horticulturists classify Japanese maple as a woody ornamental, not a tree.)

Isle Royale is located 400 miles north of Grand Rapids, and is far enough north to be two plant hardiness zones away. The list of common trees that grow on Isle Royale is shorter yet—balsam fir, white and black spruce, white pine, white cedar, aspen and birch. Less common species like the mountain ash, sugar maple and ash grow there, but only in small pockets where the micro-environment favors them. The maples grow on the warmer, south-facing slopes. The mountain ash prefers the colder, rocky outcrops. I've only seen one or two ash trees on the island.

As Mr. Kelly so aptly pointed out, the trick to becoming an expert is to become familiar with the long list of obscure insects, diseases and cultural problems that damage not only the common trees, but the lesser ones, too. Yet problems in the field rarely look like they do in textbooks. It takes a great deal of field experience to run across all of those weird, odd-ball problems which, fortunately, seldom raise their ugly heads. Only over time does one work his way up Bob's ladder of expertise. Unfortunately, when I make a mistake, like the one I made with Mrs. Tanner, I'm not taken down the expertise ladder one or two rungs. I get knocked clear off the ladder. All my credibility is lost in an instant, and the more expert I become, the higher the ladder grows. The falls become ever more painful.

Bob Kelly had no forestry degree. He was educated at what he called "The School of Hard-Knocks." After serving in the Army in the 1950s, with a stint in Panama, Bob and his wife, Trudy, returned to Grand Rapids where Bob took a job at his brother-in-law's tree service. It was the hay day of the Dutch elm disease epidemic, and what he learned was a big help when it came to teaching me how to approach the emerald ash borer crisis.

Bob shared a few other tenets he worked by. He would say, "You must go see the tree." Then, he'd repeat it. "Always go see the tree. You can't tell what's going on from looking at a couple of damn leaves someone sends you in the mail."

Words to live by.

I got a call from Mr. Davis, who owns a large manufacturing plant. He explained that his flowering crab trees were losing leaves. The call came in July, which is prime season for apple scab. Apple scab is the most common disease to afflict the apple (*Malus*) genus, which includes crabapples. The scab fungus *Venturia inaequalis* causes spots to form on the foliage in June. By mid-summer, the spots coalesce and turn the leaves brown. By Labor Day, trees are bare.

Mr. Davis said that his landscape maintenance company told him his trees suffered from apple scab and not to worry. "The disease isn't fatal and it's too late to do anything about it until next spring. They'll be fine," they told him. "Come next April, you'll never know there was a problem."

The maintenance company was right, if it was apple scab, which, over the phone, seemed likely, the trees would be fine. They were also right about treating the problem in the spring. Control consists of applying fungicide sprays in April and May. The sprays need to be done preventively, to be effective.

Flowering crabs are the most widely planted ornamental tree in Michigan, perhaps in the nation, and for good reason. They're extremely hardy. In Michigan, flowering crabs bloom profusely from late April until the end of May. Both the flowers and the tiny apples come in a wide assortment of colors. Some trees are so laden with blossoms in May that they look like a pink, violet or rose cloud. When the sun rises or sets behind a tree in full bloom, the crown glows.

For arborists, flowering crab trees are so prevalent that treating apple scab is lesson one of chapter one. I knew the people taking care of Mr. Davis' trees. "They're good arborists," I told him. "I rarely hear complaints. If you don't mind me asking, why are you calling me?"

"Because they won't come look at the trees," he said. "They told me that apple scab is rampant this year, that it's been a very wet spring, which aggravates the problem. They told me the falling leaves are a classic symptom. They're getting lots of calls."

"They never actually came out to look at the trees?" I asked.

"No, and I'm worried. They're beauties. They've got to be at least 50 years old. When they're in bloom, they stop traffic. People will get out of their cars and take pictures."

The next day I went to see his trees and could understand why he was so protective of them. The front of the property was filled with them. There must have been 60 trees. They looked well cared for, nicely trimmed, the mulch beds edged. But they certainly looked to have apple scab. Even from the street, I could see the foliage was spotty and turning yellow. Beneath each one was a growing pile of mottled leaves.

I parked in the lot and proceeded to walk through the grove, examining each tree, occasionally stopping to look at individual leaves through a magnifying glass. Every tree was the same variety and about the same age. There are hundreds of varieties of flowering crabs, but his trees were all one particular species, called Royalty crabs, which is one of the older varieties. Judging by their age, it appeared that the grove was planted when the facility was built. Founded in 1952 was imprinted on a brick by the door.

The ground squished under my feet as I walked, evidence that Mr. Davis watered on a regular basis. The grass was a deep green color, meaning the turf was well fertilized, too. The trunks and bottom limbs of the trees were stained an iron color from the well water the sprinkler system used. All of that water splashing the foliage would exasperate a fungal infection like scab.

As I checked the last few trees, something caught my eye. On the last two, and only those two, I noticed a few branches were wilting. All of the leaves on six or seven branches of the last two trees were completely brown. The branch-tips looked scorched and curled over, resembling a shepherd's crook. Apple scab may cause trees to look sickly, but it doesn't kill whole limbs. Those two trees had fireblight.

Fireblight is the scourge of the apple industry. Apple growers are ruthless when dealing with the disease. And they should be. No spray or trunk injection stops it. Fireblight is a bacterial infection as opposed to a fungal disease. Fungicides are useless against bacterial diseases, and no effective antibiotics for trees have been discovered. There are a few experimental products, but none have proven terribly successful. The best remedy for fireblight, if it can be called such, is removal. Growers cut down the trees and burn them. If the disease goes unchecked, fireblight can wipe out an entire orchard.

I went inside the facility and explained the situation to Mr. Davis. Since I was disagreeing with part of his arborist's diagnosis, I showed him pictures of the two diseases from reference books I carry with me in the truck. I pointed out how the two diseases differ.

He gave me approval to remove the two infected trees. "And, while you're at it," he said, "figure on spraying the rest of the trees next spring for apple scab."

I could empathize with why the maintenance company skipped the site visit. It's summer. They're busy. When there's a backlog of 30 calls and a dozen places to be, I, too, would be tempted to diagnose problems over the phone—not to mention hurry my examination and miss something crucial. Ninety percent of the time, maybe even 99 percent in the case of apple scab, the maintenance company's reply to Mr. Davis would have been correct. I was glad Bob had pounded into me, *You must go see the tree.*

If the temptation to hurry or skip an examination isn't bad enough, the difficulty in providing quality service should eliminate whatever arrogance an arborist might possess. The profession supplies countless opportunities to look foolish. Besides the fact that there is still so much that we don't know about trees, the basic services we provide—pruning, pest control, fertilization—are rife with ambiguities. When I prune a tree, when is the job finished? When does the tree reach that point where there's not one more branch or twig to remove? I've seen tree trimmers become so absorbed in their work, so fixated with creating the perfect tree, that before they can be dragged away, the poor sugar maple looks like a bonsai, not a shade tree. It's not exactly the look the client was hoping for.

And with no vaccinations, when is a tree cured? No pesticide eliminates pests forever. Treatments, at best, reduce problems to manageable levels and for only short periods of time. I can find an insect or fungus on any tree. None are blemish-free. At what point do treatments become necessary? When should they be stopped?

A common conversation I have with clients is trying to explain why their flowering crab developed apple scab after we sprayed it in the spring. It's August and their tree is losing some leaves. Technically, we did everything right. We applied the recommended sprays, one in April, one in May. There may only be a handful of dead leaves on the ground. But if that flowering crab is planted next to a patio or beside a front entry, the leaves are tracked into the house. Leaves may fall onto patio furniture. The scabby-looking leaves litter walks and manicured lawns.

Trying to calm a homeowner's concerns, I explain that the spring was exceptionally wet this year and that excessive amounts of moisture increase fungal infections.

"Isn't it wet every spring?" they ask.

I point out that their particular tree is one of the more susceptible varieties.

A less inhibited customer fires back, "Isn't that why we're paying you to spray them?"

I want to tell them that we could get better control if we sprayed 10 to 12 times a year like apple growers do to produce blemish-free fruit. I'd like to tell them that unless they want me to soak their tree in pesticides—and, shockingly, sometimes they do—they're better off with just the two or three treatments. I try to explain that our goal is to keep their tree reasonably healthy, not blemish-free, and that their tree will rebound next spring. I try to reassure them that apple scab is never fatal. I confess to often thinking that given the dog bombs scattered across the yard, some of which I stepped on while examining their tree, why are a few yellow leaves on the patio such a big issue? As a fresh breeze drops a new batch of splotchy leaves at our feet, I smile and suggest we add one extra treatment next year.

"Would that help?" they ask.

"It might," is all I can promise.

Everybody's picture of the perfect tree differs. Some customers prefer their trees to be "managed," which normally means they want them trimmed into a perfectly symmetrical ball or cone. They want their trees to never be sick and to only drop leaves in the fall and all of the leaves to fall into one neat pile. I once had a client set plumb lines so we could prune his cedars all to the exact same height.

Some people prefer their trees to grow wild. For them, a healthy tree is one never touched by man. For them, healthy equals natural. They flinch when we lop off a dead branch that really ought to go.

Most everyone has some preconceived notion of what a perfect tree should look like, perhaps derived from a childhood memory or storybook. In real life, the so-called ideal tree changes depending on the differing situations and varies from season to season. If a flowering crab is located at the back of a property and planted among a dozen others, a few brown leaves go unnoticed. Put that same tree where a homebound senior citizen sees it from her kitchen window, and is a reminder of her late husband who planted it, then a breakout of apple scab feels like a crisis.

It would be easy to take advantage of such people. They're desperate. Some are in tears. I could sell them summer fungicide sprays, knowing it's too late to apply them. Instead, I do my best to explain that their tree isn't dying. I ask if they'd allow me to spray next spring when the treatments will do them some good. I may suggest that we fertilize their flowering crab to reduce the stress (mostly the customer's). Fertilizing trees is a highly beneficial service, but in the case of flowering crabs, the species is so hardy that fertilizing them is primarily a placebo.

For those who were hoping for an instant solution and guaranteed results, the idea that treatments must wait until spring, not to mention that the problem is also chronic, is difficult to swallow. This is when I find out how concerned they really are.

I'm asked, "If I can't see the spots until summer, how will I know if I need to spray it in the spring? And, what if you spray next spring and my tree still gets scab?"

"If we spray your tree next spring," I say, "it might still get a little scab. But the problem should be less severe."

"Guaranteed?"

"No, I'm sorry. There are just too many variables out of our control. The sprays are only intended to help your tree stay greener longer. Think of apple scab as an allergy, like a rash. You don't eliminate allergies. You only try to control them with salves or pills or by removing the conditions that trigger the allergy."

The medical analogy often helps, but people are still likely to ask one more time, "You can't stop it? Does that mean I have to spray every year?" It dawns on them that with chronic problems like apple scab or emerald ash borer, the treatments could turn into an annual expense.

Flowering crabs, or crabapple trees as they are sometimes called, are well named. They certainly can be crabby at times. Not only do the leaves often develop scab, but if you could manage to eat a crabapple, which is incredibly sour, you'd look sour, too. The trees may be hardy, and the wood is as strong as any tree found in North America, but after emerald ash borer, crab trees may generate more house calls for me than any other tree. The whole apple (*Malus*) family, beginning with that tree in Eden—commonly pictured as an apple tree—is well known for the problems they create.

And as isolated as Isle Royale is, the island has not been immune to the apple tree problem. Dwelling on the outskirts of the Daisy Farm Campground, innocently nestled into the rocky soil at the western edge of the campground, are three small apple trees. Like their cousins the flowering crabs, apple trees are extremely hardy. In fact, they're so cold-hardy that they grow as far north as Hudson Bay. And just as flowering crabs are the most-planted ornamental tree in North America, apple trees are the most-planted fruit tree.

Nobody remembers who planted the first apple trees at Daisy Farm. But, unfortunately for the Park Service, a pair of wolves acquired a taste for the apples. Similar to the danger of tourists piling out of their cars in Yellowstone to take close-ups of the bears, campers at Daisy Farm were crowding around the apple trees at dusk in hope of snapping pictures of wolves. While there has never been a reported wolf / human incident on Isle Royale, the rangers would like it to stay that way. So for the past three Augusts—just prior to the apples ripening—the rangers have closed a portion of the busy campground to keep people away.

Knowing that interfering with wolf activity is forbidden and that Daisy Farm is one of the island's busiest campgrounds, I asked Dr. Paul Brown, Isle Royale's chief natural resource scientist, what his plan was for handling the apple tree problem.

Dr. Brown told me they are picking the apples before they fall from the trees. "We hope that by eliminating the food source, the wolves will leave voluntarily. Once the wolves figure out there's no food, they are likely to stop visiting the campground. It is highly unusual for our wolves to come so close to where people congregate. Their shyness is why some moose will live near campgrounds in the summer. We call them 'camp moose.' They find the campgrounds safe zones."

(I had noticed that and thought about telling him about the pair of moose that had copulated right behind my shelter one night and then thought better of it.)

Dr. Brown said, "We definitely want to prevent the wolves from making Daisy Farm a routine stop. Once imprinted, it will be extremely difficult to change their behavior without doing something drastic."

"Have you ever heard of wolves eating apples before?"

"No, but I haven't really looked into it."

"Excuse me for asking, but why don't you just cut them down?"

Dr. Brown pursed his lips and said, "The apple trees were recently established as a historical cultural resource."

"A what?"

"They're descendents from one of the few domesticated plants left on the island. There's currently a strong push to retain what few human artifacts remain from prior to the establishment of the park."

Dr. Brown was correct about the cultural preservation push. I'd also talked with a few of the last remaining cottage owners. With the emphasis on wilderness preservation at Isle Royale, the cottage owners are worried that people would forget about the island's human history. If the Park Service didn't retain a few buildings and artifacts, little tangible evidence would remain of the resorts or old fish camps. At the turn of the 20th century, the island was inhabited by hundreds of miners, loggers, commercial fishermen, resort owners and seasonal staff, and the comings and goings of summer visitors. If the Park Service removed every cottage, as is their practice when a private property ownership reverts to the Park Service, all vestige of past human existence would disappear.

The remaining residents have reason to worry. The end is in sight. The Isle Royale families that were granted life-lease agreements back when the park was established in 1931 are dying off. Those families were legally allowed to retain access to and use of their island property for two generations. That's almost 90 years ago now. In that time, cottage after cottage has been removed or left to deteriorate. The last few remaining cottage owners have organized, calling themselves the Isle Royale Cultural Preservation Association. They are lobbying the National Park Service to save a select number of cabins and structures.

Saving historical sites is ordinarily not a difficult decision to make for the National Park Service. For many National Parks—like battlegrounds and cemeteries—historical preservation has been part, if not all, of the reason for setting the site aside. But similar to the question of intervention with the wolf–moose controversy, historical preservation clashes with wilderness preservation. For 80 years, the park has been evolving into the wilderness I enjoy. What happens to the wilderness when accommodations for historical preservation are made?

When the island's copper and timber played-out, or became too unprofitable to procure, the island evolved into a resort and vacation destination. In the 1920s, there were over two dozen resorts scattered across Isle Royale, complete with fishing charters, hunting guides and lodges with furnished cabins.

The Great Depression not only effectively put an end to Isle Royale as a resort destination, but the demise of the resorts occurred just as there was an up-swell of public support for creating national parks. The island's isolation and unique wildlife made it a logical choice. Advocated by Michigan newspapers and state senators, as well as the island's residents themselves (which I think speaks extremely highly of the people who lived here), there was little opposition to the designation. In 1931, Congress approved Isle Royale as the 23rd U.S. National Park.

What has set Isle Royale apart from other parks was the early decision to declare it a wilderness area—a new concept at the time. In her book *Becoming Wilderness: Nature, History, and the Making of Isle Royale National Park,* Amalia Tholen Baldwin, a former Isle Royale ranger, documents why the National Park Service decided to create a wilderness on Isle Royale. Prior to this time, the Park Service's goal was to make national parks as accessible as possible, especially for the automobile. What motivated the Park Service to change its purpose at Isle Royale, according to Ms. Baldwin, was money.

In the 1920s, the U.S. Forest Service was fighting to retain its funding from the Federal Government. Seeing the surge of success the National Park Service was enjoying, the U.S. Forest Service, a far older department (created in 1881 versus 1916), decided to get into the land preservation game, too. The U.S. Forest Service approached Congress with plans to set aside a large tract of land in northern Minnesota, which would eventually become the Boundary Waters Wilderness Area.

The National Park Service had reaped international accolades for their work at Yellowstone, Yosemite and the Grand Canyon. However, by the end of the 1920s, as the Ken Burns documentary *National Parks: America's Best Idea* points out so well, the Park Service was starting to receive criticism for making the parks too accessible. Parks were becoming so overcrowded that cars were backed up for miles at entrances. Campgrounds were overcrowded. Litter and garbage abounded. The Park Service feared that their status as the agency to save America's most precious natural wonders was slipping. The U.S. Forest Service noticed their slipping reputation as well, and so applied for Federal funds to finance the Boundary Waters Area's inception.

To improve their public relations and maintain funding, the National Park Service decided they better change their mission slightly, and get into the wilderness-preservation game, too. It also couldn't have gone without notice that the proposed Boundary Waters Area was located practically across the lake from Isle Royale.

In her book, Ms. Baldwin records that she had the privilege of interviewing one of the last commercial fishermen to call Isle Royale home. The late Milford Johnson and his brother, Arnold, along with their families, had lived on the island for decades. They commercially fished the near shore waters since before the park's inception, particularly the north shore. Interestingly, Milford Johnson told Ms. Baldwin that for him the island felt wilder before it became a park. He said, "I think it would have been more of a wilderness then than it is now. Much more."

It's a curious observation. He was comparing the island now to a time when large tracts had been clear-cut, when the commercial fishing industry thrived, and when island residents came and went. Considering Isle Royale is now a 99 percent federally designated wilderness area, to me, Milford's remarks felt like a contradiction.

The Johnsons fished out of Crystal Cove, not far from where I normally stay on Belle Isle. I never met Milford Johnson, but I'd seen his wife hanging laundry outside their home in the 1980s. I was new to Isle Royale at the time. My first trip was in 1982. I viewed the island as wilderness in extremis. Seeing bed sheets and undergarments hanging from a clothesline was my first introduction to Isle Royale as a place with a human history. I was to find out later it was a history that reached back thousands of years. Excavations have revealed Native American copper mining that dates back to 6,000 years ago.

There's no one left who commercially fishes Isle Royale any more. The license expires with the resident. To me as a sports fisherman, the absence of that firsthand knowledge about the lake and its fish seems like a great loss.

On the other hand, I am certainly grateful the Park Service set aside Isle Royale as a wilderness. It should be said that the few remaining residents are also thankful, despite the eventual loss of their cottages. I've heard several say they would've hated to see the island turned into a place where only the wealthy can afford. They know the shorelines would have eventually mushroomed with pricey vacation homes and all of those private property signs that go with them.

That the park rangers won't cut down the apple trees because of their historical value testifies to how serious they take their responsibility to the few remaining residents. That they pick green apples is also testimony to how serious the rangers take their responsibility to the wolves and the wilderness status of the park.

The landowners' proposal to retain a few cultural artifacts has gone through the formal request process. Consistent with their philosophy of allowing limited, controlled human access on Isle Royale, the Park Service has decided that when the time comes they will save some cottages but remove most. I think the apple trees will eventually go.

I do hope that one of the wolves' trots off with an apple and its seeds are planted somewhere secret, a place that only the wolves know about. Every land should possess a few trouble makers. And apple trees are perfect for the job.

Dorothy (Johnson) Stegman is one of the last living residents to overwinter on Isle Royale. For two winters in the 1930s, she and her two older sisters attended Isle Royale's one-room schoolhouse. After reading my first book, *Naked in the Stream: Isle Royale Stories*, Mrs. Stegman called me to get some advice about writing her memoir. On the phone, we agreed to meet at a bookstore in Grand Rapids where her daughter lives. Mrs. Stegman brought with her some family photo albums to show me. To my delight, the album contained old photos that are a treasure trove of island history. We sat together at a table for over two hours, sipping tea, and leafing through photograph after photograph. She showed me several pictures of the park's dedication ceremony held at Rock Harbor in 1941 and pictures of the Civilian Conservation Corps (CCC) work camps from the 1930s.

The CCC work crews were there to help clean-up downed-brush from a previous logging operation. They also saw firefighter duty during the great fire of 1936, when one-third of the island was burned. Mrs. Stegman's mother and father and sisters all worked at the camps. She said they cooked meals and washed clothes and acted as guides. She said that the money the family earned came in "real handy."

I asked Mrs. Stegman how it felt to be the only women working in a camp on a remote island holding 300 men. "Were there any problems?"

She said she was only a little girl then and that her older sisters and mother had done most of the work. She never heard of any trouble and seemed surprised at my question.

One album contained a photo of her dad and a group of men she said she didn't recognize. They were all posing beside a buck-pole. She thought the picture was taken around 1915. From the buck pole hung nine wolves. Lowering her voice to a whisper, she told me. "Those were different times."

Mr. Haadsma owns 20 acres of woods on the outskirts of Grand Rapids, Michigan. His property and home are located in an ambiguous zone of real estate that's neither rural nor suburban, and certainly not urban. His property is close enough to town that he can drive into the city to work and not feel as if he's spending half his life on the road, but far enough away that he feels as if he's making an escape. He considers his twenty acres of woods a little paradise. It's where the sound of the highway still drones in the distance, but he no longer needs to raise his voice to be heard when the family gathers on the patio.

Mr. Haadsma called me to have his woods inspected. Because tree inspections mean different things to different people, I ask clients like Mr. Haadsma, what they hope to achieve? Do you want your woods managed for timber production, to create wildlife habitat, maybe both? Do you want to create a park-like feel to your land, where the undergrowth is cleared out so you can walk unencumbered? Do you prefer leaving it natural?

"Is there anything specific you want me to help you with?"

I like to know what motivates a person to go to the trouble of picking up the phone to call.

As it turned out, Mr. Haadsma wasn't interested in growing timber, though when I mentioned his trees could be worth some money, the thought did give him pause. He eventually replied, "No, I'm not really interested in harvesting my trees and definitely not looking to remove all of the underbrush." He paused for a long time, struggling to put into words why he called.

I rescued him with, "Do you basically want to know if your trees are healthy?"

"Yes. That's it," he said, obvious relief in his voice. "That's exactly what I want to know. And," he added, "Is there anything I should be doing toward that end?"

Mr. Haadsma isn't alone. Lately, people have been requesting something new from their tree service. They want to know how healthy their woodlot is. Mr. Haadsma is in a growing number of knowledgeable property owners who understand that their land has gone through dramatic changes. They understand that their land was clear-cut at some point in the past. They realize that the stumps were likely dynamited and burned so as to create a pioneer's homestead. The original farm has faded away, too. The land has now evolved into a patchwork of old fields and woodlots. Many of the property owners are also aware that invasive species pose a real threat to their trees.

Mr. Haadsma's request for a simple tree checkup is actually a reasonable one.

But I think his request goes deeper than that.

Only two centuries ago, nearly all of the Midwest was forested. Those trees have all been removed. The re-growth has been cut also. People don't own a virgin forest anymore and they know it. What little is left of old growth trees was set aside long ago in small preserves like Hartwick Pines. Yet, despite being well aware that their land has drastically changed from those pioneer days, many people still hope that their little section of forest might one day return to something that resembles pristine. They hope that one day their woods will return to a certain type of vitality. It's the kind of vitality that I see on Isle Royale.

The problem is, of course, it takes many decades to grow a healthy, vibrant forest, not to mention a lot of work. With all of the changes made to their land, Mr. Haadsma realizes that without some help, there is little hope his woodlands will ever return to anything that resembles a virgin forest. The changes to the land are so sweeping and widespread that, in fact, nobody is sure anymore what forests will evolve into—even if they are left undisturbed for decades.

I enjoy talking with landowners. They are interested in hearing about their trees, and they tend to want to do what is right. Most clients are also realistic. They are pragmatic people. After a short conversation, they quickly grasp that they need to settle for growing a healthy, sustainable woodlot versus trying to recreate virgin forests. The question they then ask me is, "What is a healthy forest?" That is a difficult question to answer. The water we drink may be healthy, but we understand that it's tainted. We purify the water to "acceptable health and safety standards."

The soil supports life, but has been worked and reworked.

Today's trees no longer tower over us. Our notion of what a tall tree is has even changed. I can't count the number of times someone's asked me to remove a 30 foot pine because it was "getting too big." Their notion of a tall tree is forty or fifty feet. When a tree reaches sixty feet, I'm often asked if the tree has reached its full life expectancy. "Shouldn't we remove it before it starts to die?" they ask. They are surprised when I tell them that a fifty foot maple or oak has just reached puberty, and that even a hundred foot pine is still fairly young.

Some enterprising naturalists in Kansas tried to recreate a small portion of the former Great Plains by growing a few hundred acres of tall-grass prairie. They tilled the ground, tried to purge the soil of non-natives and planted the appropriate seed and waited. Despite their best efforts, what resulted was a combination of native grasses and invasive grasses and weeds. The soil biology had changed to such a degree that they were unable to recreate the lands the Kiowa, Osage and Sioux hunted.

Grasses grow fast. In theory, one should be able to recreate a tall-grass prairie about as quickly as establishing a good lawn. A prairie should be far easier to recreate than an old growth forest. Their failure does not bode well for growing the forests our nation once knew.

Thirty years ago, I rarely received a call to address forest health. I was asked to check individual trees in people's yards, but not whole woodlots located well outside of town.

Most landowners who live near cities no longer think of their acreage as a commercial venture. They are not timbering their property nor farming it. Their land is more valuable to them with the trees than without, for the resale value of their property is more than double with the trees. Besides, they aren't looking for their land to produce a cash crop anyway. They have jobs. They work hard as engineers or doctors or grind out enough hours in a factory so that their property doesn't need to produce a cash crop.

To help Mr. Haadsma better understand what he wanted, I become the equivalent of a real estate agent. Instead of showing him pictures of Dutch colonials, Victorians and Cape Cods, I show photos of climax forests. I show 8 x 10 glossy pictures of mature woodlands, where the sunlight slants through the canopies of hundred-foot maples, beech and hemlock. The trees stitch a lacework of leaves and branchlets that tower above a forest floor covered in trilliums. I show photos of conifer-stands where the ground is blanketed with the equivalent of a thick comforter worth of pine needles. The pictures display moss and lichen-coated fallen branches. You can almost smell the pine scent.

I once had a client ask me not to step on any of the moss in his woods. He'd lived in downtown Chicago all his life. He'd invented the computer mouse and made enough money from his invention to never need to work again. He'd bought a parcel of forest land across from the Interlochen Arts Academy near Traverse City. Every inch of his wooded property seemed precious to him. He practically tiptoed through the woods as we looked at the property together. I obliged him by being careful where I stepped, but couldn't help but think it would be tough to levitate trucks onto his property to do tree work and wondered if he expected us to airlift out the wood and brush so he could build his driveway and home.

Fortunately, I did not find any invasive plants. If I had, it would have meant going to war, and wars are messy ... and expensive. There is collateral damage. If the woods are full of invasive plants, the eradication process will be violent. Removing large trees or even understory plants is not a gentle procedure. His woods would look mangled when we were done and his forest wouldn't resemble anything near pristine for many years.

Without them being able to say so, I believe what landowners hope to accomplish is to not only grow a healthy woodlot, but to nurture their woodlands to recreate what's been lost. "Pristine" may be the best word to describe what Mr. Haadsma wants. He wants his 20 acres of forest to look something like a national park. A big part of my job is to change his expectations and gently bring him back to the new reality.

We can dream about living in a land that's never been touched by man. But similar to explaining to Mrs. Smith that without taking extraordinary measures, we can't make her flowering crab blemish-free, Mr. Haadsma needed to learn how to settle for healthy—and healthy is often difficult enough to achieve.

I can help him grow a vibrant, sustainable 20 acres of trees. As for creating virgin forest, he will need more than I can deliver. My promising anything more leads only to disappointment—his and mine.

Isle Royale is as wild and as native a habitat as can be found in the Midwest. Being surrounded by the largest of the Great Lakes certainly helps. What little pollution there is has blown in on the wind or remains from the previous century. But it is not absent of human mistakes. It is not wound free. Even Isle Royale needs a helping hand at times. That's why I pack my pruning saw.

The rangers guard the perimeter with a religious zeal. I don't know what they will eventually decide to do about saving the island's wolves or keeping the apple trees. They might introduce wolves. I think they are likely to remove the apple trees. But for the most part, I'm guessing the Park Service will allow nature to take her course. As I understand it, letting nature take its course is the goal. As such, the national park people tend to take the long view here. I'm not sure I always agree with their position, but understand why they hold that stance. I do admire their courage. It will not always be a popular course.

As an arborist, who doesn't work on lands anywhere near as wild as Isle Royale's, I know that a non-interference approach is a luxury I don't possess.

I'm glad they feel they still have that option. I'm glad someone does.

THE ROOT OF THE MATTER

"We live on a planet that has a more or less infinite capacity to surprise. What reasoning person could possibly want it any other way?"

~Bill Bryson

THE BIOLOGY OF TREES IS AN EPIC ADVENTURE TALE THAT'S FULL OF SURPRISING twists and turns. The closer one looks at how trees grow or the ecology that surrounds them, the more fascinating their story becomes. And if you want to listen to a tree tell a great tale then Isle Royale is the place to be. The forest here stretches from one tip of the island to the other. Even the tiniest of outer islands—sometimes no more than a rock that breaks the surface of the lake—grows trees. They're stunted, miniature versions, but trees none-the-less.

Back home, they actually pay me to listen to what trees have to say. I have the pleasant task of noting a slight change in a shade of green, or a sickly branch-tip. I'm actually paid to give them my full attention. And I try to listen closely.

As a result, I'm always looking up. It is not an uncommon event to trip over objects right at my feet because I'm staring at the treetops. My shins are perpetually healing from some bruise or scrape. The upside is that a day rarely goes by that I don't see raptors soaring overhead or watch a crane lumber by, or admire an unusual cloud formation. Seeing an eagle soar never grows old. The job as an arborist definitely has its perks.

Few people are paid to listen to trees, and it's been my observation that for most other people, when they think about trees, it's normally to enjoy their shade while sipping a favorite beverage on their deck. Many people appreciate them while walking a woodland path where the forest seems to put life's concerns into better perspective. At the other end of the spectrum are those who barely notice trees until autumn. They may admire the blaze of color, but they also shake their heads after their trees drop a Saturday afternoon's worth of work onto the lawn. It is no coincidence that autumn is when the tree service receives its most removal requests.

I think it safe to say that for most of us, not a lot of attention is paid to the intricacies of trees, and it is also safe to say that even less attention is given to their roots. Tree roots tend to be an out-of-sight, out-of-mind subject. But the trees would tell us if we listened that their roots are vitally important and something we definitely should not take for granted. When a homeowner asks me to inspect their sick tree, one of the first things I want to know is if the roots have been disturbed. Is it a new transplant? Has there been any excavation done recently? Has anything unusual been poured into the soil? If the entire tree appears weak, there is often a problem underground.

Knowing how important roots are, the plant pathologists at the Morton Arboretum, located just outside of Chicago and one of the most well-respected tree research stations in the world, are doing a great deal of research on tree roots. The Morton Arboretum holds bi-annual symposia for root scientists, who travel from across the globe to attend their workshops. These symposia are titled, "The Landscape Below the Ground." I'm no root scientist but I have attended a couple of the conferences as someone wanting to learn more about trees. One of the more revealing insights uncovered by the Morton scientists is that tree roots exist much shallower in the soil profile than was once believed to be true. The plant pathologists say they discovered the shallow nature of tree roots while seeking an answer to a very simple question, the question being:

"Where are the roots?"

I confess I hadn't given their exact location a whole lot of thought, presuming they're somewhere under the tree. But once the question was asked, I realized that I didn't really know. If there was such a thing as a soil x-ray machine, what would the pictures reveal? The Morton people set out to find an answer.

After carefully excavating hundreds of trees situated in almost every possible habitat—urban trees, forest trees, tropical trees, conifers and deciduous, trees grown in sand, grown in clay, trees growing in nurseries, and century old giants—the pathologists discovered that approximately 90 percent of any tree's root system is located within the upper 24 inches of the soil. And over 50 percent grow in the upper 12 inches. The tiny feeder roots are shallower yet. They're located in the upper six inches. Very few, if any roots, grow below two feet deep.

Another surprising revelation was, minus a few rare exceptions, there is no such thing as a taproot. A tree's root system does not mirror the tree's crown as is so often pictured in the older biology books. There is no trunk-like taproot pushing downward with root-limbs growing from it, and smaller root-branches spreading further downward, with the root hairs being the equivalent of leaves growing as deep as the tree is tall. A root system does not mirror the crown. Nor does the sum of the wood in a root system equal the mass of the wood above ground. Depending on the tree species, the roots can easily be less than 10% of an entire tree's mass.

An accurate depiction of a root system is a wide, shallow dish that holds soil and roots. Root zones resemble a pancake in shape. It's a pancake of earth and roots and micro-organisms that radiates outward from the trunk and extends to the drip-line and beyond. Many root systems extend horizontally twice as far as the branches reach.

Few people besides the Morton researchers have picked up a large tree to look beneath it. I was lucky enough to be part of a team of arborists hired to move two large trees at Grand Valley State University in Allendale, Michigan. The largest was a 45-foot-tall silver maple with a trunk diameter of 16 inches. The other was a 14-inch-diameter ash (prior to the emerald ash borer infestation). The two trees were in danger of being sacrificed to a building expansion project. Dr. Arend Lubbers, GVSU President at the time and noted tree-lover, was interested in saving the maple and ash. He was able to procure funds to finance their move.

The job required several pieces of heavy equipment—cranes, dozers, backhoes—and a week's worth of careful excavation to retain a sufficient size root ball. Calling it a root "ball" is a misnomer. It was more like a root-rectangle. Following the Morton Arboretum's guidelines, we dug each hole, 3-feet-deep and 16-by-20-feet-wide.

According to the crane's scales, the tree, the soil, and the raft of steel pipes that we drove beneath it so as to lift everything, weighed 76,000 pounds. The weight surprised us. We'd calculated it to be half that. But it had rained hard all that week, and the soil was saturated. So much so, that we almost lost the first crane. When it tried to hoist the tree out of the hole, an out-rigger caved in. The shocked, "Oh No!" expression on the operator's face as his mega-ton, mega-expensive rig suddenly shifted was a look I will not soon forget.

A bigger crane was brought in. When it hoisted the maple and then the ash, we found no evidence of roots at the bottom of the 3-foot-deep holes. I have seen many smaller trees transplanted and can verify what the pathologists say. Few roots are located at the bottom of a transplant hole. Instead, the majority of the roots fan across the upper few inches of soil. Ten years after we moved the university trees, they are still alive and doing well. No signs or plaques mark their auspicious journey. Walking by them, you'd never know they survived a major transplant.

For the Morton researchers, finding where tree roots are located entailed the cautious removal of tons of soil. It was painstaking work. It's much like the tedious work archaeologists do with soft-bristled brushes, gently sweeping away the earth and debris from rare artifacts. In my opinion, the plant pathologists' work brought to light knowledge as ground-breaking as any archeologist's dig. And similarly, it took the pathologists a while to fully understand what they'd unearthed.

The original question the pathologists had asked was, "Where are the roots?" And as odd as it may seem, apparently nobody knew. The discovery that tree roots are located in the upper two feet caused them to scratch their heads. For it begs the question, "Why?"

Wouldn't roots anchor a tree better if they were deeper? Wouldn't they reach a more consistent and dependable water source? If tree roots are so shallow, how do they support such large plants? How can such a shallow root system anchor a tree that weighs many tons and sometimes leans at a 45 degree angle or more? Many trees outweigh homes. The General Sherman sequoia weighs an estimated 1,500 tons. That's comparable to holding nine houses off the ground on a single central pillar that sways in the wind.

To adequately answer the *why* question, the pathologists at Morton Arboretum felt they needed to first answer the *how* question. How do trees determine where to grow roots. While investigating, they discovered something else. It turns out that tree roots are "advantageous." If you water a seedling on one side of the flower pot and not the other, the roots will concentrate in the watered half, which only makes sense. But the roots originally grow in every direction. Finding no water in the dry half, those roots atrophy and die. To compensate, plant hormones trigger it to send extra roots into the watered half. That so-called "trigger" explains why once a tree root finds a septic line, the roots practically race through the pipes.

For the scientists, the idea that a tree tells itself to grow extra roots in the watered half only emphasized the mystery. That must mean a tree "decides" to grow roots in the upper two feet of soil as opposed to below that level. Again, what's so special about the upper two feet?

Perhaps school kids could have answered their question. Every schoolchild is now taught that trees absorb carbon dioxide and emit oxygen. As early as the second or third grades, students are taught that trees are vitally important to the planet. Given the well-documented recent rise in atmospheric CO_2 levels, I'm extremely thankful the lesson is being taught. Perhaps the next generation will be more motivated to make significant changes to our energy consuming ways. What they don't mention in school, however, is that tree roots exhale carbon dioxide and inhale—or absorb—oxygen. It is the very opposite of what the leaves do. That doesn't mean we need to change what we teach our children for the leaves far out-produce the roots.

Plant pathologists already knew that tree roots need oxygen and that without enough oxygen plants die, which caused them to wonder if maybe the shallow nature of tree roots had something to do with oxygen levels in the soil. When they tested for oxygen at varying soil depths, the deeper the tests were performed the less air they found. The reason was the weight of the earth on top of itself. The deeper you go, the more earth there is compressing down on the soil. More than two feet deep, the earth compresses the soil so much so, it literally squeezes the air out of the air pockets between soil granules. For those roots below two feet, it would be like trying to breathe with an elephant sitting on your chest.

Breathing is nature's most critical life support issue. Plants are no different than animals. If the air, water and food supply is all cut off at the same time, plants die far quicker from lack of air than they do from lack of water or food. It explains why an over-watered houseplant wilts within an hour. The plant isn't suffering from an over-dose of water. The plant is suffocating.

The fact that tree roots need to breathe also helps to explain something that had puzzled me for a long time. Trees thrive in the rockiest of terrain and in the sandiest most porous of soils, but not in a bog. It's a fact that's most apparent in locations like Isle Royale, where trees grow atop bare rock. Trees also thrive along the Lake Michigan's eastern shoreline where the largest freshwater sand dunes in the world exist. Water runs through that sand like a sieve. Yet those dunes are covered in forests.

In a swamp or marsh, where there is several feet of moist black earth, few trees grow. It had never occurred to me that the reason trees struggle to live in bogs is that they can't breathe.

There are exceptions to that rule, of course, as there are exceptions to almost every biological principle. Certain trees like mangroves thrive in their namesake habitat, mangrove swamps. Many of their roots do live above the water, but many roots are also submerged in sea water. The salinity levels alone would kill every tree on Isle Royale. And even in the north, certain trees like willows and alders are able to tolerate long periods of high water levels.

If needing to breathe wasn't reason enough for tree roots to prefer the upper two feet of soil, the Morton people also noted that trees prefer to "dine" at the very top of the soil profile. Indeed, their excavations revealed that most (90%) of the tiny feeder roots clung to the upper two-to-four inches.

Roots anchor a tree. They absorb water and air. But they also feed. It should be said, the words "feed," "food," and "eating," are misleading. Trees don't actually consume soil. If you bring a houseplant home, it will not suck the pot dry of earth. Instead, by "feed" we mean the roots and soil exchange chemical compounds.

And Isle Royale is a place loaded with so-called tree food. You can't take a step without stepping on someone's meal. The forest floor is where countless discarded leaves and decaying plant and animal matter fall. The organic matter is a treasure trove of tree food. Farmers have known for centuries that organic matter is crucial for growing healthy crops. The scientists at Morton Arboretum knew it, too, and it didn't take them long to connect the dots. If most of the organic matter lies within the top couple of inches—and it does—then that's where feeder roots want to be.

All of that rich organic matter would go to waste, however, if roots didn't get a little help. Without the assistance of soil micro-organisms, most, if not all, of the nutrients from organic material would be unavailable. It's the micro-organisms that breakdown organic matter into food that trees can digest. These tiny soil fungi, bacteria, nematodes and insects are the equivalent of soil chefs. They mix and cook all of that debris into a proper diet for trees. The cooking process is why standing piles of mulch steam. And trees are very fussy about who does the cooking. I'd go so far as to say that trees only want their mother to cook for them, and no one else.

For trees, as for us humans, home-cooked meals create a wonderful aroma. Pick up a handful of healthy earth—earth that has been well mixed, oxygenated, and digested by all of those wonderful micro-organisms—and hold it to your nose, and the earth smells rich and sweet, almost wholesome. Pick up a handful of "dead" earth, where all of the microbes have died, with little oxygen, and the soil smells putrid.

Oddly enough, these are the same organisms that cause me to cringe when I find them inside the house. The "work" they perform is why we work so hard to sanitize our kitchens. They cause food to rot, an old sofa to smell, and my wife to throw away my favorite shirt that I refuse to part with. Yet when these same micro-organisms are placed on the forest floor—where they belong—they not only cook up some great tree food, they actually clean up after themselves. Without fungi, bacteria and the rest, the breakdown of the world's dead leaves, twigs and fallen trees, not to mention dead plants and animals, and their feces, would have to wait for physical friction to break them down. That friction would have to be supplied by wind and water erosion or someone's feet.

Tree roots require oxygen. Soil microorganisms require oxygen. Oxygen lies in greatest abundance closest to the surface. For the Morton people, it explained why tree roots are so shallow. And as so often happens when trying to answer a seemingly simple question, other important discoveries are made along the way.

There is a class of micro-organisms called mycorrhizae that attach themselves to tree roots. They form a symbiotic relationship with roots, and when the two marry, the mycorrhizae wrap a tree root with the equivalent of a superpower body suit. The fungus grows billions of tiny cilia. Cilia are microscopically small hair-like structures similar to root hairs—only far smaller. Cilia reach into places root hairs can't. When these cilia lend their support, they multiply—many fold—a tree's ability to grip the earth and to breathe, to drink, and to feed.

Beneficial soil microorganisms, like mycorrhizae, hold some of the greatest promise for repairing over-worked soils. They are already being used to help clean up toxic waste sites. If beneficial soil organisms could be cultured, grown for production and safely introduced, one could theoretically sprinkle a few spores onto a field or a homeowner's yard and produce a Garden of Eden effect. Unfortunately, finding the right strain of beneficial fungus or bacteria for each plant species (the microbes differ for each) is a daunting task.

The biota must also be tested to ensure they don't wreak havoc. Placed where they don't belong, they could overwhelm already present beneficial organisms.

These super fungi make me wonder if I took home a bottle of soil from Isle Royale—something not allowed—and sprinkled the earth around a client's tree, would I unleash a giant beanstalk-effect? The island's microbes have been allowed to develop undisturbed for over 80 years. Are they special? Have they grown in power?

There is one nagging question left unanswered. How do such shallow roots manage to anchor a tree?

To that question, I've never heard or read a satisfactory answer—at least not to my satisfaction. When I examine a blown-over tree, the roots don't normally break. Instead, the tree pulls over the plate of earth with it. Unless the roots have rotted, the soil gives way before the roots do. The roots have so thoroughly stitched their way throughout the soil that you can't separate the tree from the earth it's anchored to.

Which causes me to smile.

Trees belong to the earth. They are interconnected, and I didn't understand or realize how literal that connection is. It explains why I feel a loss when a tree is removed or dies. Something feels out of place. It's like when a friend moves out of town or passes away. I don't just miss them. I also miss the way everyone else behaves around them.

*

Unlike the previous year's American Society of Consulting Arborist's conference, this year's event is taking place in a location that's similar to Isle Royale. The hotel sets beside a very cold, deep lake. The lake is in fact over a thousand feet deep. That, however, is where the similarities end. Lake Tahoe is surrounded by snow-capped mountains and multi-million dollar homes. They are mostly summer homes which are largely deserted at this time of year, except for the skiers who come here to take advantage of the area's ski resorts.

It needs to be said that, as an organization, the American Society of Consulting Arborists has a knack for finding great keynote speakers. Last year, Dr. Haas tackled the subject of making big decisions. He urged us to do our due diligence, and he opened our eyes about procrastination in the name of wanting more information.

This year's keynote speaker is "Treetop Barbie." She is standing beside the moderator waiting to take the podium. The moderator is going over a few housekeeping items for this year's conference such as the perpetual reminder to turn your cell phones off and an encouragement to attend the social events, which most of us need little encouragement to do. (The first two drinks are free.) When finished with the announcements, the moderator tells us what a privilege it is to introduce this year's speaker and commences to go into a five minute description of her career. I'm thinking, *Just let her speak.*

"Barbie" smiles at the description of her career and then looks down. She glances up when she hears herself called by her nickname and, thankfully, smiles again. I couldn't help but wonder if she would be insulted at the Barbie Doll reference. She must have a good sense of humor, for when she finally does take the podium, she acknowledges the applause, and after thanking the emcee, the very first thing she says to the audience is, "I prefer the name, 'Queen of the Forest Canopy.'"

She then lowers the microphone so she can be heard more clearly for, unlike the perspective I have of Mattel's tall, statuesque Barbie, Treetop Barbie stands only 5-foot-4 and has brown eyes and auburn hair. She explains she was tagged with the nickname by her research assistants, who work beside her in the tops of 300-foot Douglas firs. She also tells us something we, as arborists, already know. There are few women who work in our trade, and even fewer who climb trees for a living, which certainly adds notoriety, as well as my respect for her.

Her real name is Dr. Nalini M. Nadkarni and she is a forest ecologist for Evergreen University in Western Oregon. Forest ecology being the broad topic it is, Dr. Nadkarni narrowed her field of study to tree canopy habitats and the plants that grow there. Her base of operations is located in the State of Washington where some of the tallest trees in the world grow.

I try to attend as many tree care conferences as I can for I never feel like I know enough about trees. There's not a day that goes by that I don't see something that completely mystifies me, and the consulting arborist conferences are my favorites. Dr. Nadkarni has been featured in *National Geographic Magazine* and The *New York Times,* and is a recipient of an Emmy for her PBS specials on forest canopies. She was at our conference to lecture on the importance of habitat preservation. At a conference for arborists, who would well understand the importance of maintaining healthy habitats for trees, she first appeared to be preaching to the choir. What made her message pertinent for me, however, was that she is successful at preserving forests, and on a grand scale.

She told us she likes climbing trees. She said that weighing only 90 pounds proved to be a real asset. Being so light it enables her to reach branch tips the men can't. Her assistants joked that she's so light she'd probably float to the ground if she fell. I weigh far more than 90 pounds and I know firsthand how being light would be an asset to a climber. Once while pruning out flower galls near the top of an 80-foot ash tree, Don Kooiman, a more experienced tree pruner and a Michigan tree climbing champion no less, cautioned me: "Don't place your weight too far out on an ash limb. Ash gives you no warning when it's about to break. It doesn't groan or creak like other woods do."

Moments later, foolishly testing his advice, I ventured too far and without any warning there was a loud crack and I dropped like a stone. I'd have plummeted 60 feet to the ground had I not been well-secured by my climb line, falling 12 terrifying inches before the rope caught my fall.

Still, despite the risks, I've always liked climbing trees too, and could relate with Dr. Nadkarni's joy for climbing. It takes some getting used to, but once I overcame my initial fear of heights and trusted my equipment instead of gripping the tree like a frightened cat, working aloft feels as exhilarating as it sounds.

Dr. Nadkarni explained how she'd turned her two passions, tree climbing and her love of nature, into a career. She'd acquired her undergraduate degree in biology from Brown University and her Ph.D. in forest ecology from the University of Washington. As part of her doctorate program, she set up viewing platforms in the tops of giant western hemlocks and Douglas firs. Her first canopy stations, she told us, were crude rafts of borrowed planks set in place with old ropes and cables. The wealth of information she soon gathered, not to mention her jaw-dropping, *National Geographic* quality photographs led to enough financial backing to build a much-improved research facility in Olympia National Park and build a second station at Monteverde National Park in Costa Rica.

Of all the beautiful panoramic treetop photographs she showed us that day, and of all the insightful preservation methods she used, it was her unique approach to research that stayed with me. She told us she approaches research in reverse. Normally, a scientist takes a theory or supposition and tests the idea's validity through a rigorous series of experiments. Dr. Nadkarni says she does the opposite. Starting with no particular supposition or conclusion, she first asks a question that wants an answer. She said those answers lead her to ask more questions that lead her to more answers and so forth. She meticulously records the data as she goes. She readily admits to this odd research approach and offers no apologies for it. Tongue in cheek, she says, "If you don't like it, then climb on up and we can discuss it."

Little sunlight reaches the ground in old-growth forests. The only way for ground plants to find enough sunlight is to hitch a ride on a tree. With no soil to establish their roots, tens of thousands of plant species, most of which had never been studied or named before, found a way to take root in the tops of trees. One of the first questions Dr. Nadkarni wanted an answer to was, "How do these plants take root when there's no soil?"

The aerial plants, called epiphytes, are not parasitic to their hosts. She explained that they have developed the ability to filter nutrients from the blowing mists and fogs via cilia-like hairs on their leaves and stems. As the epiphytes live, die, and decay, they build a layer of biomass around the tree limb. This rich, organic biomass becomes so fertile that the epiphytes establish a more normal root system, and that the tree limb will even sprout roots into the material. "It's almost," she said, "as if the aerial plants are returning the favor of providing a habitat for their parent tree."

Following her curiosity-mode style of research, she made two discoveries that propelled her career into the limelight. One: she discovered that canopy ecosystems are very delicate. Two: ferns, mosses, lichens, bromeliads, orchids, and the rest of the epiphytes take a long time to become established, a minimum of 20-to-25 years. She discovered this when she wanted to see what would happen if she stripped a section of epiphytes from a limb. Like a small child dismantling a toy only to discover they can't put it back together again, she discovered epiphytes don't re-grow overnight. Given the moist, fertile-appearing environment, she'd expected to practically watch the moss and ferns re-sprout before her eyes. When little happened after 10 years, it became clear that her treetops were decorated with delicate antiques.

She told us that her secret to success was that she diligently quantifies her data, and documents all of her findings. Recording all of the information is what distinguishes her curiosity-driven research from mere conjecture. Several times during her presentation, as evidence, she used graphs, photographs, and diagrams to demonstrate how she reached her conclusions.

Good timing also played a part in her success. Just as she was finding answers to how plants thrive at the tops of trees, the rest of the scientific community was answering why we should care. Scientists from around the world were measuring increasing amounts of atmospheric carbon dioxide. They were also watching the ozone layer thinning over the poles. The health of Dr. Nadkarni's delicate treetop plants looked to be a canary in a coal mine. Since tropical forests provide constant carbon dioxide/oxygen conversion, she found herself right in the middle of—or at the top of—the planet's atmosphere experiment station.

Dr. Nadkarni told us that as her career skyrocketed, grants and endowments arrived in her university mail-slot weekly. She was getting pulled in a hundred directions, spending most of her precious treetop time answering questions at Senate hearings, giving presentations to science foundations, and speaking at conferences. She wasn't able to do justice to the field work anymore. Feeling obligated to take advantage of her new-found status, she turned over the canopy research to her team of scientists so she could give full attention to preserving tropical forests.

With the help of a Guggenheim Fellowship awarded in 2001, she created a whole string of environmental protection organizations. She founded the International Canopy Network, the Research Ambassador Program, and the

Legislators Aloft Program. The last gives lawmakers an opportunity to climb a tree (with help) and take a bird's eyes view of the forest. The program allows them to feel the mist on their faces. They get to experience a world where life exudes from every pore. Tree-protection laws soon followed.

Dr. Nadkarni has designed a canopy camouflage clothing line. She has written and produced a host of books, articles and films, and said she shamelessly sold as many Treetop Barbie dolls as she could. All the proceeds went toward forest canopy preservation.

I listened closely to Dr. Nadkarni's remarks, not just because I found the topic fascinating, but because I was also hoping for some answers of my own. My efforts to preserve habitats were struggling.

In the early 1990s, West Michigan enjoyed a housing boom. It was heady times for the building trades, and many prospective home buyers preferred building on a wooded site as opposed to an open field. Wooded lots were in such high demand that many sold for more than twice what tree-less properties cost. Unfortunately for thousands of new homeowners, two-to-five years after they moved into their home, their trees started to die. I began receiving more calls for what arborists call "construction disease" than for any insect or disease problem.

The dieback at one development was particularly severe. It was a thickly wooded parcel, called Maple Woods, and located beside the Grand River, the largest river in Michigan. The parcel contained trees that thrive in occasionally flooded areas where rivers overflow their banks. Red and silver maples, ash and elm, cottonwoods—all prefer heavy, wet soils. The homeowners complained enough to the developer about their trees that he called me to see what was wrong.

With him at my elbow, I examined each tree, and it quickly became apparent that the die-off had nothing to do with insects or some new pandemic. I told him I also saw no evidence that the trees had been poisoned, which had been his suspicion. (Apparently, there had been some protest to his developing the land.) I explained, as we walked, that the ground had not been poisoned. If the soil had been poisoned then the undergrowth and lawns would also look sick, which they didn't. "Besides," I told him, "you'd have to be pretty ambitious to individually poison so many trees." There were at least a couple hundred dead trees, and more that looked sickly—most of them right next to the street.

I took a deep breath and steeled myself.

"Mr. Howard," I said, "the reason your trees are dead is because you killed the tree roots."

I'd learned the hard way that it was best to be direct with developers. Don't mince words. Normally, developers, builders, and contractors appreciate a straightforward approach. With that said, I waited to see if I'd pissed him off.

Hesitating, he said, "Go on."

I pulled out a sheet of paper, placed it on the hood of my truck and began to sketch a crude blueprint of a typical residential street.

"This is why the trees are dying. As you know, John, the normal easement for residential streets is sixty-six feet wide. Most builders remove all the trees within the right-of-way. They clear-cut the entire 66-foot easement so they can more easily build the street and bury the utility lines.

"You only cleared a thirty-foot-wide swath for your streets. I presume you did that because you were trying to be more environmentally sensitive as well as financially prudent. Is that correct?"

"Well, yes. Why not? People like the trees. It's why many of them bought the lots."

"Here's the problem." I said. "Tree roots are only two feet deep ... or less. When they trenched for the utility runs, they trenched three foot deep as required. By digging three feet deep, they sliced through most of the roots."

A twinge of doubt crossed Mr. Howard's face.

"I know. It's hard to believe that roots are that shallow," I continued, "but it's true. Tree roots do not grow deeper than two feet. All the studies verify that. Most roots, in fact, are shallower than that, yet, especially in a flood plain such as this."

As I penciled out the street, I said, "Tell me if I'm wrong. The road itself is twenty-six-feet-wide. Now you didn't do it here, but some plats even add four-foot-wide shoulders. Right?"

"Yes."

"Your utility lines for the plat are buried in trenches that run beside the street. The public utilities—gas and electric—are placed in trenches ten feet beyond the edge of the street on both sides. The private utilities—telephone and cable—are placed in a second trench that's ten feet beyond that. Private utilities aren't allowed in the same utility corridors as the public utilities."

Mr. Howard said, "We have to bury the lines instead of going overhead with them, which is a good idea. Who wants to look at power poles and wires?"

"Yes, I understand, and agree. But, unfortunately, by burying the utilities in four corridors beside each street, you sliced through all the roots of any tree within twenty feet of the road.

Mr. Howard's face was turning ashen.

"To make matters worse," I explained, "when the excavators removed 12-inches of topsoil for the roadway bed, they replaced the topsoil with sand—as required. They then pushed all that heavy alluvial topsoil to either side of the street and then graded it smooth. All of that heavy equipment running back and forth over that earth compact the soil, and squeeze the air out of it."

"But they have to do that to build streets and roads." Mr. Howard said.

"Yes, they do. You're right. But as backfill goes, clay, which is the predominant soil type here, is very unforgiving. Clay has only tiny air-pockets between each soil particle. Clay particles are 500 times smaller than sand particles, which doesn't allow for many air pockets."

To his credit, Mr. Howard was listening patiently. But some doubt still showed on his face.

I pulled out one my favorite analogies to help him grasp the situation.

"The importance of soil particle size can be compared to a McDonald's playroom where children submerge themselves in four feet of plastic balls. There's so much air between the balls there is no fear the children will suffocate. Tree roots that grow in sand or loam soils, or even un-compacted clay, are like the McDonald's playroom. In those soils, there's enough air between the soil granules for roots to breathe. Compacted clay, however, is as hard as concrete— harder in fact. There's actually more air pockets in concrete than compacted clay. It's why they use clay to line retention ponds."

Reality was beginning to settle in. But as a last gasp effort, Mr. Howard complained, "But the street is six years old. The trees only started to die recently."

"That's the sad part," I said. "If the damage isn't too severe, healthy trees can survive for five years on their stored sugars. But once those sugars are depleted, typically 2-to-5 years later, and well after the contractors are long gone—the trees die.

"Mr. Howard," I said. "I'm really sorry. But sliced roots, a soil with no oxygen, your trees never stood a chance."

Mr. Howard asked me to attend a meeting where he quickly assembled his sub-contractors. At the meeting, he was understandably upset. "Someone should have told me," he shouted. And despite everyone in the room being well-respected architects, engineers and excavators, none of them had ever heard before that tree roots are so shallow.

Several of his subs questioned my diagnosis, many of them were convinced I was wrong, not an unusual response.

As a result, I though something needs to be done. These are intelligent, often time kind people. They're just unaware of the problem is all.

As the politicians say, "I went out on the stump." If arborists didn't start to speak up about this, who else will?

I began to write articles for the local trade journals. I gave countless tree preservation workshops at the Home Builders Association. I hounded the builders, architects and landscapers, preaching to them about how tree roots are shallow and how to avoid killing trees. I carried the torch of urban tree preservation to people I thought could make a difference. It was exhausting, time-consuming work, and my efforts appeared to have little impact. The trees in West Michigan continued to die needlessly.

Dr. Nadkarni had my respect. If she could convince legislators to save entire forests, why was it so hard for me to teach builders how to preserve a single tree?

After the contractors left that meeting, Mr. Howard and I met for drinks down the street at the Shawmut Inn. He looked so disheartened that I told him I'd buy the first round. He had hoped his people would be more receptive to the *education.*

I'd expected their reaction and told him so. "Give them a little time," I said. "They'll come around. Now that they know what to look for, they'll start to notice how trees die where grades are changed or roots cut."

Taking a sip of his Crown Royal, he said, "I hope so."

"You might not think it, but it'll be the excavators who come around first. They're always digging. They see the roots. They become some of the most ardent believers."

We sat there silent for a while.

"Vic," he said after a long pause, "I almost forgot. My mother wants you to look at her tree."

"Sure ... what's up?"

"I don't know. But it's looking rough. My wife and I built her a home on a lot she liked because of the big beech in back. We graded her backyard since she wanted all the humps and bumps smoothed out. She'd really hate to lose that tree."

He looked up at me and quickly dropped his eyes. I think we both knew what the problem was. I inwardly groaned. No tree is more sensitive to root disturbance than the American beech.

I finished my beer and we shook hands. "I'll take a look," I told him.

*

The Morton Arboretum scientists had simply wanted to know where the roots are.

Dr. Nadkarni had wanted to know how plants take root in the tops of trees.

Even Dr. Haas only wanted to know why wildlife scientists drag their feet.

It seems everybody has that one question they want an answer to. The search for an answer quickly evolves into a thousand other questions, many of which hadn't even occurred to them before.

I, too, had wanted an answer to a question. I'd wanted to know why so many trees were dying in new developments. I'd suspected the reason was root-related. I rarely saw any above ground damage to the trees. It was the reason I'd attended the Chicago symposiums. My tree preservation efforts had started shortly after seeking that answer.

I couldn't help but wonder: Was there a save-the-planet movement down every Q & A trail? If I study spruce adelgids long enough, will I look for a cure for cancer? If I study the influence that trees make on the psyche, will I urge hospitals to place pictures of trees in patients' rooms? If I study construction damage long enough, will I end up standing on a stump to preach?

It appears so.

Perhaps that explains why young children go through a period where they ask "why?" to every answer we give them. They continue to ask why until we tell them to stop. Maybe we shouldn't.

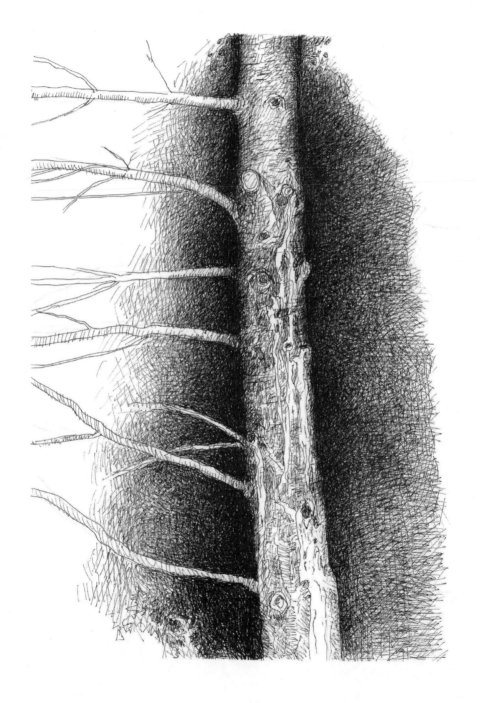

IGNORANCE IS NOT BLISS

"I pulled up on shore and gathered driftwood and laid it in the bottom of the canoe. I'll be warm tonight. Nothing burns better than driftwood."

~Foerster's Isle Royale Journal

AFTER MORE THAN 80 YEARS OF CAMPERS SCAVENGING FOR FIREWOOD ON ISLE Royale, the campsites are picked clean of anything that resembles dry wood. Park regulations prevent the cutting down of standing trees. And with no deadfalls or dead limbs close at hand, some people resort to snapping off live branches. More than once, I would watch campers roll into Belle Isle and immediately go searching for firewood. Soon I'd hear the crack of live tree branches being snapped. I winced at each snap. Later that night, when I heard them struggling to get their campfire lit, and then coughing from all the smoke that burning green-wood creates, I thought it more than poetic justice.

Breaking off a live limb by brute force leaves a terrible fracture. It's a wound that will never heal. I became so tired of seeing all the splintered, frayed branch stubs near my favorite campsites that one year I packed-in a folding pruning-saw to repair the jagged wounds.

Few people pack a saw to the island nor should they. Ken, the friend I normally go to Isle Royale with, scolded me for carrying an extra pound of what he thought was useless weight. He laughed while watching me try to "prune the forest." I suppose I did look foolish. But the fractures are a terrible injustice to the trees. A wilderness area should look wild, not ravaged.

In a sense, the book on tree roots reads like a mystery novel. What exactly is the transaction that takes place between a root hair and a soil particle? By breaking down the myriad of chemical, physical and biological factors involved in the tree root/soil exchange, might I learn, chapter by chapter, how to plumb the earth for a wealth of minerals? Could I then design a root-like osmotic sponge, throw it on the ground and retrieve all the minerals I need, gold included?

The story of photosynthesis is an epic saga about one of nature's greatest wonders. How does something as small as a leaf convert three of the most common ingredients on the planet—sunlight, water and carbon dioxide—into complex sugars that produce miracles like apples or walnuts or maple syrup?

What lies within the heart of an acorn that somehow finds that elusive spark of life?

How does a pinecone seed that weighs less than a gram, no heavier than a snowflake, grow into a giant?

They all have a story to tell.

Yet despite the mysteries that trees could resolve for us, most "tree" research dollars go toward commercial ventures such as growing better fruits and nuts or...wood. And while at first glance, the book on wood may not have the glamour of searching for the spark of life or tapping the mineral riches of the earth, wood has its own fascinating tale to share.

For many people, when trees come to mind, they don't think about a tree. What first comes to mind is what we use trees for, and, when it comes to using trees, their wood is at the top of that list. Foresters, carpenters, builders and craftsmen have studied the multi-faceted properties of wood for centuries. They've tested each species for tensile and load strength. They've looked at decay resistance, grain patterns and wood density. They've studied how different types of wood absorb stains or paints or repel water. And which burns better. For much of the world—especially visitors to Isle Royale—trees mean fuel for campfires and cooking.

Arborists, on the other hand, want to know how wood heals.

When I swing an axe and slice open a tree, I create a wound. If I miss and slice open my leg, instead, I also cause a wound. Trees and people heal in different ways. When I cut myself, antibodies and white blood cells are rushed to the wound to fight off infection. The tissues surrounding the wound begin rebuilding what was lost. Our bodies actually have the ability to replace tissue. If the injury isn't so large as to leave a scar, evidence of the accident eventually disappears—other than perhaps a mental scar and a lesson learned about being careless with sharp tools.

Trees, however, cannot replace tissue. They may grow new wood, but not replace what was lost as we do. Tree cavities never refill. Nor does tree sap contain antibodies or white blood cells. Instead, a tree fights off an infection by sealing-off the wound. They box it in. They construct walls around it. The tree uses its own wood as a construction material and nature's original carpenters erect cellular barriers that stop infections from spreading. Dr. Shigo, a renowned forestry pathologist, calls this healing process "compartmentalization."

When I met other campers, I sometimes mentioned that I make my living as an arborist. Those who knew what an arborist is often ask if I'm one of those people they see clearing power lines or doing tree removals. I explain that our company doesn't trim for the power company, which requires special training and classifications, but we do remove and prune a lot of trees. Tree removal and pruning make up more than half of our business, and, as a result, we are often asked for the wood. In Michigan, many people still burn firewood to heat their homes. Winters are long. Free firewood is a real money saver. Typically, if we leave any wood on a job site, it will quickly disappear. If it's oak or cherry, it may be gone by the end of the day.

I recently attended a tree pruning workshop by one of the country's foremost tree experts, Dr. Tom Smiley of the Bartlett Tree Research Institute. Dr. Smiley told us—and he may have been complaining a little—that there's money to be had for studying fruit trees or coffee trees or trees for timber or pulpwood production. But due to insufficient funding, studying how trees heal is often a primitive affair. Dr. Smiley then described a study he and his assistants had undertaken to determine the reduction rates for wind loads on pruned vs. un-pruned trees. It has long been believed among arborists that pruning trees reduces the risk for storm damage. I have sold many pruning jobs to homeowners based on that premise.

To confirm that pruning trees really did reduce wind loads, Dr. Smiley stood nursery trees upright in the back of his pickup and secured them so they wouldn't blow over. He then hooked a tension meter to the trunks and used the truck's speedometer to clock wind speed while he motored down the two-tracks in the nursery fields. Readings were taken before and after different types of pruning and at different wind speeds. He said the chore of watching the tension meter, a device that measures wind pressure in pounds per square inch, was assigned to an unlucky intern who sat in the bed of the truck and shouted the meter readings to the driver as they rattled through the fields.

Dr. Smiley found that wind loads were reduced by up to 25 percent for the pruned trees. His team also found that it didn't matter how they pruned them. They wondered if there'd be any difference if the trees were trimmed correctly— thinned appropriately, and the dead and broken branches removed—or if they just whacked the tops off. He found that any method created the same wind-load reduction. Not surprisingly, the most important factor was how much of the tree was removed. Dr. Smiley paused briefly, before telling us that this was in no way an endorsement to prune trees however we felt convenient.

The study helped to show that pruning does indeed reduce storm damage to trees, and confirmed how important pruning can be. Statistically, far more injuries occur to people due to falling limbs than from the fall of an entire tree, as was the sad case with the husband from Kalamazoo.

Tree pruning, however, comes at a cost, and not just to our pocketbooks. Each time we cut off a limb, branch, or twig, we create an open wound. Dr. Smiley's closing admonition to not prune trees however we felt convenient was good advice, for there is definitely right ways to prune and definitely wrong ways. Incorrect pruning cuts rarely heal.

There are times when this is all-too-apparent.

One spring, I received a call from a summer youth camp to investigate why an anchor tree for a high-ropes course toppled over. A high-ropes course is an obstacle course of elevated tightropes, suspended rope ladders, balance beams and Tarzan swings that are sometimes built among the canopies of large trees. The idea behind the jungle gym in the sky is to teach kids courage. A child wears a safety harness connected to cables that run above the course. The lines attached to the safety harness are then belayed to a ground-person, who can safely lower the child if she falls or panics and freezes. I was told this course was suspended about 25 feet off the ground.

When I discussed the toppled anchor tree with Dave, the camp director, he told me over the phone that when the staff returned in the spring they found the tree uprooted and lying on its side. It had evidently fallen sometime during the winter. The tree's fall caused him concern about the rest of the trees in the course.

Dave explained that children had been coming to the camp for many years. He said the high-ropes course was a big attraction, and successful completion had become a rite of passage. All week, counselors would work with groups of kids to teach them how to trust one another. The counselors talked to their kids about how to overcome their fear of heights and how to rely on their equipment and trust their belay person. And how to stay focused while performing in front of a large audience, which was sometimes the hardest of all to overcome. Everyone attending the camp would gather at the course for the week-ending high-ropes event.

After hanging up, I couldn't help but think that the fall of an anchor tree did not bode well. A tree as important as an anchor tree should never uproot. Something felt amiss, and I was glad he called. I certainly would go evaluate his trees, despite the camp being more than a hundred miles away.

As it would turn out, he would never have needed to call if he'd had the privilege of listening to the Father of Arboriculture.

Fifty years before Dr. Smiley's wind-load study, Dr. Alex Shigo, pioneered the study on how wood heals. Dr. Shigo was a New England forestry pathologist for the U.S. Forest Service. And if Dr. Smiley's research tools seemed archaic, then Dr. Shigo's were practically prehistoric by comparison. He said he basically used three tools—a hatchet, a bottle of iodine, and an old microscope or magnifying glass. The iodine wasn't used as an antiseptic, but as a stain to better see wood cells through his microscope.

Dr. Shigo's research entailed making several types of wounds to live trees and then watching how they healed. Having hundreds of square miles of U.S. Forest lands to work with, he said he made tens of thousands of wounds. He made gashes. He made clean cuts. He snapped off branches. He caused ugly frayed, splintered cuts. He drilled holes. At the conference where I listened to him speak in the late 1980s, near the end of his prestigious career, he told us that at times he felt like a little boy turned loose in the woods with his first hatchet.

Dr. Shigo said he returned each year to monitor how well the trees healed. By chronicling the type of cuts he made, the location, the length of time since the injury, and the extent of healing, he noticed there were distinct trends.

When he cut off a limb too long and left a stub, the pruning cut barely healed, if it healed at all. When he cut off a branch too short and removed the branch collar, the wound also didn't heal properly. But … when he pruned off the branch just outside of the branch collar the cuts healed three times as fast. When he told us this, he pounded on the podium with a fist and shouted, "Three times as FAST!" Even a difference of one inch up or down the branch he said proved vital.

Branch collars are the swollen rings of wood shaped somewhat like a donut that are located where a limb attaches to the trunk or the branch to its limb. The donut-shaped ring of wood is swollen because it's where the two woods—trunk and limb—weave together. With every passing year, dual rings of sapwood merge. Over time, they form the equivalent of a plywood type of connection. The two grains crisscross each other, as well as intermixing.

These wooden unions are incredibly strong and hold tremendous amounts of weight. With no guy wires, trusses, or other means of support, tons of wood are held in the air for sometimes centuries. Ship builders used these unions, called knees, as bracing for their hulls. And as every lumberjack knows, cutting through one is a losing battle. The union wood—or "crotch" as the woodsmen colloquially call it—is so hard an axe bounces off it.

What Dr. Shigo wanted to know, however, wasn't why branch collars are so strong, but why they heal cuts so much faster than elsewhere on a tree. He would eventually learn the reason is due, in part, to the dual layers of sapwood located within the branch collar. The extra sapwood compounds the tree's ability to grow new wood. It grows three times as fast, a point he made crystal clear.

When Dr. Smiley warned us to prune correctly, he was referring to the pruning guidelines set forth by Dr. Shigo. At the time of Dr. Smiley's lecture, they'd become well-accepted standards throughout the industry. They are still the guidelines we follow today.

Most of Dr. Shigo's research occurred in the 1950s and 1960s. His work revolutionized how we care for trees, and earned him among his peers the title of "the Father of Arboriculture." He also studied several other tree health matters, including pruning paints, wound dressings and sealers. He was able to show that paints, stains and tars—no matter what the substance—had no effect on preserving live wood. The previous thinking was that if wood preservatives helped lumber resist decay, then it was only logical that paint would protect pruning cuts. A few of the cuts on the trees in the ropes course were painted. But similar to using concrete in tree cavities, paints, stains and concrete inhibit the wood's ability to create its own natural barriers.

The bad news for the early tree surgeons was that Dr. Alex Shigo's study showed how much of their previous work was ineffective. I still run across a few old trees that one of my predecessors filled and/or sealed with concrete. Trying to remove one is near impossible. For those of us doing tree pruning since that time, Dr. Shigo's discoveries have been met with cheers and partying. Like logging, tree pruning is one of the most dangerous professions, ranked second only to commercial fishing based on workman's compensation rates. Liability insurance is far higher for tree workers than for firefighters or police officers. Part of the "danger" has been the weight of the equipment tree trimmers needed to transport up a tree. The old model chainsaws are twice as heavy as the new models. The "better" tree trimmers used to cover all of their cuts with tree paint, not an easy task eighty feet up a tree. For the guys in the trees—it was strictly a male profession in those days—Dr. Shigo lifted a gallon of paint from their work belts.

✳

After the two-hour drive north to the youth camp, it felt good to step out of the truck and stretch my legs. It was a cool morning, but sunny. A fresh northwest wind carried cold, damp air off Lake Michigan. The chilly breeze caused me to zip up my jacket. During the colder months of winter, I often wear dark colored pull-overs to soak up the sunshine, taking advantage of any heat the sun offers. On the day I visited the ropes course, I didn't need to wear black. With a little bit of walking, I'd warm up soon enough.

The youth camp was set in rolling dune-lands, where smooth-crowned hills were covered in mature hardwoods. It's the kind of terrain and forest that borders much of Lake Michigan's eastern shore. A green blush tinted the hills. Buds were beginning to swell on the undergrowth. A few dandelions bloomed where they grew against south-facing walls.

Finding the office building, I knocked on the door and walked in. Dave, the camp director, greeted me. There was no whistle hanging from his neck, but he carried a clipboard and an air of authority, which I'm sure came in handy for managing a campground full of children and young adult counselors.

"Mr. Foerster," he said with a smile, "It's very nice to meet you." He stepped forward to shake my hand. "Appropriate name, if you don't mind me saying so."

He had a firm handshake. "Good to meet you, too, Dave." When he finally let go of my hand, I was glad to have it back. "It's why I normally introduce myself as Vic. It avoids the explanation that I didn't change my name for the job."

Dave nodded as if he understood. Turning to the reason for my visit, he said, "Vic, I'm glad you're here. But I'm terribly busy this morning. Several contractors are on site today, and I don't dare stray far from the office. Being your first visit here, you're going to need some help finding the high-ropes course. I'm going to have Sarah drive you out there."

Dave picked up a phone on one of the desks and placed a call. After hanging up, he said, "She'll be right over."

Ten minutes later a young woman walked in and introduced herself, as Dave had already gone off with a cement contractor. Despite being only twenty-three years old, Sarah also seemed a confident sort, as if she too was accustomed to corralling teenagers. Her friendly intelligent face was fringed with wind-tossed, blondish, red-tinted hair.

She pointed me to her car parked out front and told me to set my tools (rubber mallet, wood chisel and binoculars) on the backseat. When she turned the key, the car sputtered to life. Placing it in gear, she backed out, and soon we were on our way. The Saturn's old springs squeaked over each bump on the two-track we followed, and I couldn't help but think that camp counselors probably don't make much money. I hoped her car would survive the short trip.

We quickly struck up a pleasant conversation. She had a contagious optimistic outlook on life. More than once she told me, "You have such a cool job." She also told me the camp here was "great," and she "loved" all the staff. She talked about how she enjoyed the "awesome woods."

The narrow lane we traveled would not cause me to disagree with her. The lane meandered through a stand of mature pines and then through oak, maple, and beech woods, and then more pine. I noticed that between many of the trees were scattered, flat-topped stumps. Judging by how little rot there was to the stumps, someone had done a selective-cut no more than five years before. The loggers had done a pretty clean job, too. There was no sign of the tree tops that are typically left behind. There wasn't even drag marks where they'd skidded the logs out. Hopefully, the camp made a little money on the timber sale.

The two-track emptied into a graveled parking area, which was fairly large and felt more like it belonged in front of a grocery store than in the middle of the woods. A sign at one end of the lot pointed to the path that led to the course.

"Hope you don't mind a little walking," Sarah said. "The ropes course is still about a half-mile from here. You'll see the tree when we get there. It's pretty obvious. I'm surprised it didn't pull more trees down. It's gonna be a real chore to repair it and have it ready to go by next month."

After driving the two hours to reach the camp, I thanked Sarah for the opportunity to do some walking. We set out down the path at a brisk pace. By now it was mid-morning and the day was starting to warm up. She walked ahead of me, looking back every time she stepped over a fallen branch to make sure I noticed it.

She kept up a steady stream of conversation, sometimes with me, sometimes with herself. "I suppose we'll have to redo the whole thing," she said aloud. "Brad and Tom and Morris, they'll be up for that. They're rock climbers. Those guys love this kind of work. I suppose you guys must do a lot of climbing." Not waiting for my reply, she said, "Yes, they will enjoy this."

I didn't mind her running dialogue. Most my days are spent alone or filled with talking to other tree guys. Today, however, was a refreshing change of temperament—no griping about the weather or work conditions. There was no talk of last night's nefarious conquests or staying out too late.

After about a 20 minute hike, we walked over a low rise and emerged from the woods into a small clearing. The land gently fell away into a shallow bowl. In the center of the bowl was the ropes course. When we broke through into the clearing, Sarah said, "Here we are."

I'd been paying attention to the ground at my feet, and I didn't look up until I walked a few paces into the clearing. When I did, I stopped short.

Sarah walked a few more paces and then realized I wasn't following any longer. She turned around and was about to ask what was wrong when she saw the expression on my face.

I tried to reply to Sarah's questioning look, but no words came out. Spread before me, not 100 feet away in the center of the dell, was an acre-size grove of "trees." One huge tree lay on its side, uprooted. Snapped cables and ropes dangled from the adjacent trees, evidently breaking when the anchor tree went down.

What had stopped me short were the remaining trees. They had all been topped. Every single tree in the course had been sawed-off just above where the highest lines were set—maybe forty feet high. And they weren't just topped. Every single limb had also been removed. And to compound the indignity, all of the bark was peeled off the trunks, as well. The entire grove contained de-barked, de-limbed, naked, 40-foot tall tree trunks. The trees had all been turned into poles.

Standing there in the April sunshine, I felt a cold shiver wash over me. I could envision the hundreds, maybe thousands, of children who had navigated these suspended ropes, swings, and ladders. I could picture the excited kids and their counselors milling about beneath them. Parents, who had come early to pick up their children, were cheering below, lending encouragement. I could almost feel the intensity of a young girl trying to gather her courage to timidly step out over the void. On wobbly legs, she slides one foot out on a now trembling tight rope.

The tree supporting the tight rope has finally weakened to the breaking point, and the added weight of a sixty-pound girl causes it to snap. I can hear the dry, brittle trunk fracture, then crack in two. The tree wobbles, cables sag. The crowd suddenly falls silent. The tree teeters harder—one way, then another— and then it falls. The terrified young girl dangles in mid air as her belay person screams for help.

Slowly at first, but gaining a terrible swift momentum, one tree falls and then another and another. The cables and ropes attached to each tree pulls over its neighbor in rapid progression, domino fashion. Counselors, not knowing which way to run or who to save first, realize too late that everyone is about to be enmeshed beneath a network of cables and ropes and lines, and crushed by tons of falling timber.

I shudder again, and manage to weakly say, "Sarah, we need to go talk to Dave."

Neither of us spoke until we were halfway back to the parking lot. Pushing past a low hanging branch across the trail, Sarah finally risked asking, "Vic, what's wrong? Why did the tree fall over?"

I'd been trying to work out my upcoming conversation with Dave, and I didn't realize she was speaking to me at first.

Sarah asked again, "Mr. Foerster, what happened? Are you all right?"

I stopped walking, turned around, and collected myself before saying, "Sarah … the roots on every one of those trees are dead. They've completely rotted away. Why on earth did they cut off all of the limbs, and … strip off the bark?

"I don't know," she said with a puzzled look on her face, not yet understanding the implications. "It's been like that since I started working here."

I tried again. "Sarah, those trees, they are no more than logs stuck in the sand, and not stuck very deep either. I doubt the trunks are set more than 12-inches in the ground."

Sarah placed her hand over her mouth.

"Yes, Sarah. That's right. The camp has been incredibly fortunate. How long have you worked here?"

"About six years," she said finding her voice. "It was the summer after my junior year in high school. Yes, six years."

I felt goose bumps rise on my arms again.

Back at the office, I waited outside while Sarah found Dave.

I hadn't thought of a more tactful way to begin, so when he arrived, I walked up to him and said, my voice trembling a bit, "Dave, you have to shut down the high ropes course."

"What? Why? What's wrong?" Dave's smile faded.

"All of the trees are dead. Why on earth did you cut off all the limbs? Even the bark has been removed."

I'd caught him off-guard. So I allowed him a moment to digest my recommendation. "Dave," I continued, "Live trees are not utility poles. For the life of me, I can't understand what the thinking was. This has to be one of the most dangerous situations I've ever encountered."

He swallowed hard. Clearing his throat, Dave said, "We had an old caretaker who used to tend the grounds. He's retired now. Said he once worked as a logger in New England. He told us if we removed the limbs, there'd be no risk of them falling on anyone. So we did."

"The bark?" I asked.

"Well, the bark started to slough off after a couple of years. He suggested we skin the trunks as well. That was a really long time ago ..." his voice trailed off. The gravity of the situation was beginning to dawn on him.

I placed my hand on his shoulder and said, "Dave, let's go inside and talk."

We went into his office and he closed the door behind us. The three of us sat there in silence for a long while. Dave and Sarah's faces looked haggard.

I began by gently explaining to them how trees grow—that their roots are shallow, not to mention necessary. I talked about how wood heals, how a tree needs bark to retain its sap.

I told them that I could come back in two weeks with a crew to help them set up a new course—one set among living trees with healthy roots, where only the dead and broken branches are removed.

He quickly agreed.

Mulling over the near-disaster during the long drive home, I thought about how managing all of those kids would be a challenge. Nurses, teachers, counselors—it's a lot of responsibility. People like Dave and Sarah impress me. Children demand your full attention. Maybe that's why they'd missed what I saw as so obvious. Or maybe I was being too kind. I shook my head. It wasn't the first time I'd heard of a supposed "tree-guy" giving bad advice.

I cracked my truck window open. The cab had grown warm from the sunshine. The fields and woods along the highway seemed to flow by. The snow in the shadier pockets of the woods was gone, not to return until next winter. I looked for deer in the open fields, searched for wildflowers. The juneberry trees were starting to blossom.

I turned on the radio, but wasn't paying much attention to the music. While driving along in the pleasant spring haze, it struck me. Ignorance is not bliss. Today had been a good day.

MOVING FORWARD

"There is always now ... always."

~Eckhart Tolle

Broad, smooth rollers steamed across Lake Superior and, even from half a mile away, I could see the waves swell, curl and spill over the outer reefs. The winds had calmed at dawn, but Isle Royale's north shore was still feeling the brunt of last night's storm. Superior does not lay down easily. The waves continued tumble offered fair warning to mariners to stand clear. There are hundreds of shoals and barely submerged reefs beneath the near-shore waters of Isle Royale. The reefs have caused the demise of many a stout ship. Between the heavy fogs of spring and November's gales, the island's toll on watercraft has been substantial.

The rumble from the distant surf was loud enough to mute the birdsong at Belle Isle, and as the sun crested the Greenstone Ridge, the first rays of light stroked the tops of the diminishing waves, as if the sun was trying to calm Superior. Last night, there'd been no rain, no thunder, no lightning. But sometime during the night, the winds had switched from west to the north and freshened to 25-to-35 knots. Whether it's raining or not, if you're in a boat that much wind classifies as a storm. If you're in a canoe, that much wind feels like a hurricane. Fortunately, there was no need to canoe this morning. And despite the wind's roar in the trees last night and the surf's rumble, I'd slept like an Isle Royale rock. I was now sitting high and dry at the picnic table, sipping at a mug of hot coffee, watching the start to another beautiful day break across Robinson Bay.

The first thing I do in the morning, after making coffee, is to sit down for a few moments to study the lake. There's something about the water that draws your eyes. Though from where I was sitting, the trees were starting to block the view. I shifted over so I could see more clearly. One day those trees would permanently block the view of the lake, maybe not in my lifetime, but possibly my children's and certainly my grandchildren's. I'd been coming to Isle Royale for over 30 years and often stay at Belle Isle. For thirty years I'd watched the trees get taller and fill out. Much like my family, they were growing up.

A hundred years ago, there were no trees where I sat. They'd all been removed. My picnic table might well have been positioned in the middle of a fairway. Old photographs show that a putting green had been located not 50 feet from the "wilderness" shelter I'd slept in. When Fred Schofield built his Belle Isle resort near the turn of the 20th century, to better compete with the other resorts, he added a small golf course. Mr. Schofield cleared away the rocks, all of the trees and stumps, and then barged in earth and topsoil from McCargo Cove. He graded the area using horses and plow blades, contouring the land into its present shape. He then sowed grass.

After the resort closed in the 1920s, the turf was no longer mowed. The golf course quickly evolved into an open field, and all evidence of the golf course—other than the grass—has slowly disappeared. The Park Service has demolished all of Mr. Schofield's buildings but for one, an open-air pavilion that remains today.

For several decades, the grass at Belle Isle out-competed the trees for space. But, Michigan being Michigan, the trees are making a comeback. The surrounding forest is encroaching on the field. There are now several young trees scattered across the site. Some trees are as tall as 40 feet. The field's demise, one of the few remaining open fields left to Isle Royale, is inevitable. It made me wonder if the Park Service would consider removing trees to improve a view. Would their mandate to allow the park to grow wild trump protecting a vista for campers to enjoy?

Trees grow.

It's one of the most basic tenets of arboriculture, and also one of the most overlooked. Every time I see someone plant a tree beneath a power line or underneath a home's eaves, I shake my head. It is one thing to knowingly plant trees with the intention of removing them when they outgrow their space. It is quite another to completely forget that one day they may stand 100 feet tall. There is something about the march of time that makes even the most intelligent person slip into denial. With that said, I've also found that my senior citizen clientele are all too aware of the creep of time, and it strikes me as a little sad when an 80-year-old asks, "What's the biggest tree you can plant?"

The first timber men to the Great Lakes Region skipped over Isle Royale. They were primarily looking for white and red pine. Logging operations began in the region in the early 1800s and tapered off toward the end of that century to its present pace. The early loggers liked pine because it grows straight, tall and fast, and is relatively light. Pine floats high in the water, which made the logs easy to float downstream to the mills, many of which were located at river mouths along the Great Lakes. Before the invention of the gasoline combustion engine, land transportation was either horse-powered or via trains. The water routes made moving logs far easier and cheaper than trying to haul tons of wood overland.

The forests of Isle Royale primarily consist of spruce and fir, but not the giant spruce and fir that grow in the Pacific Northwest. Isle Royale's trees are white and black spruce and balsam fir. They grow straight, but not tall or very fast. They would have been a poor investment compared to pine. Also, barging rafts of logs across Lake Superior to the mainland mills presented obvious challenges. Rafts could span acres in size and are the equivalent of trying to haul icebergs. Any amount of wind would thwart the strongest of steam-powered barges. As a result, only a third of Isle Royale would ever be logged, and much of that to build the mine camps and resorts on the islands themselves.

At Belle Isle, there is a nice white spruce that grows right beside my shelter. The shelter overlooks a picturesque cove and faces east. It's a perfect place for watching the sun rise over the Greenstone Ridge. The spruce is 25 feet tall. It's thick and full, and has a healthy green color with no dead limbs. It would make an ideal Christmas tree for a mall. But it must have been a tough summer because the spruce grew only two inches this past year. Four inches would be considered a good year, judging by the growth rate between the terminal bud scales of the previous years. Using three inches as an average, that would make the 25-foot spruce 100 years old.

The trees that grow right along the Lake Superior shoreline are windswept and gaunt. The cedar trees, in particular, are so stunted that they appear to be screwed into the ground. The bark spirals counter clockwise down the trunks in tight slanted swirls. Cedar grows slowly and Isle Royale's cedars grow exceptionally slow—about an inch per year. The ones right beside the lake grow slower yet. Despite some of the cedar being a couple of hundred years old, the biggest trees measure only 24 inches in diameter at their base, and only 12 inches in diameter at eight feet high. I'd need a magnifying glass to see the paper-thin growth rings. On Isle Royale, a 25-foot cedar growing along the lake may be over 400 years old.

In the rest of the Midwest, by the end of the 19th century almost every tree had been removed. Consequently the current "oldest" trees are only around 120 years old. And even 120 is a stretch. Most of the land has been cut more than once. When my forefathers first arrived to Ontario in the late 1700s—later transplanting to Michigan—the trees they found were three centuries old, some were older. By those standards, today's oldest trees are at most, middle-aged.

Some foresters would say the trees on Isle Royale are over-mature, and in a sense, they're right. The heartwood is starting to decay and there's a lot of storm damage—busted tops, broken limbs. The trees will soon be a poor investment. Foresters want clean, solid wood from top to bottom. Even a small pocket of decay can drastically reduce a tree's value. The logs quickly go from veneer to crate-wood.

As an arborist, I prefer to see trees reach full maturity. From an arborist's point of view, a little trunk decay is fine as long as the tree doesn't pose a hazard. And if a hollow tree is in the middle of the forest where few people venture, then let the hiker beware. Few natural wonders feel more like a cathedral than ancient forests do. If you've never walked a needle-covered path beneath the canopy of virgin pines or seen the Pacific Northwest—go! Don't wait. And when you go, be sure to get out of the car and walk down the trail. Walk until you no longer see the parking lot. I suggest walking off trail. Immerse yourself. Then … go a little farther.

Clients often ask me how old a tree is. I don't know if people are curious or if they want to know whether their tree has reached full life expectancy. Are they looking to justify removing it? The question feels a little intrusive to me. With rare exceptions, the trees within the cities are, at most, 80 years old, which surprises some people. Not knowing any better, they think their tree is some last vestige of the original forests. But it wasn't until the 1920s that people became interested in planting trees for more than fruits or nuts. Searching old photographs from that era, it's difficult to find more than a dozen trees left standing in an entire town. Tree planting didn't come into vogue until citizens realized, too late, that they needed to correct the rampant soil erosion. A forest canopy dampens a rain's pounding. Without that canopy, the exposed forest floor washes away. Soil quickly erodes into streams and lakes. In the towns, the dirt streets and people's yards were one big mud puddle after a storm.

Due to their centuries-long lifespan, trees can be used as barometers for measuring annual atmospheric, soil, and weather conditions. The thickness of the growth rings and length of annual twig growth will, minimally, tell me whether a year was a good growing season or not. By taking assays of wood cells inside each growth ring, the levels of heavy metals and carbon dioxide can be measured for as far back as the tree is old. Certain species can live for a thousand years and more, and have been used to pinpoint dates for volcanic eruptions, droughts and forest fires.

Case in point; a couple of years ago students from Hope College in Holland, Michigan, were helping the Great Lakes Water Research Institute perform air and water quality tests. The institute was taking lake-bottom samples from Lake Michigan, and they were delineating the sediment samples into the equivalent of annual growth rings. Each layer of sediment represented years, and then decades, going back to the fourth century B.C. The timeline stopped when the researchers reached bedrock. To help confirm the more recent data, the institute hoped to use local trees to double-check their readings. They wanted trees at least 500 years old.

I heard about the project somewhat by accident. A retired oil company geologist who lived in the Holland area called me looking for some advice. He lived on the lake near the off-shore project. The geologist wanted to know whether I could determine the age of his trees without cutting them down to count the rings, something he preferred not to do. He told me the students had contacted him at the suggestion of their professor who was a friend of his. The professor knew he owned several old trees.

"Wood cores could be extracted," I told him. "But if there's a tree you don't mind sacrificing, it might be better to remove it rather than turn it into Swiss cheese. Taking cores is not as easy as it sounds. And … perhaps you're unaware of this, but … I doubt you have a tree that's older than 100 years."

As anticipated, he was a little surprised until I reminded him of our state's logging history, particularly right along the lakeshore where moving logs was easiest.

We had a nice phone conversation. Both of us were interested in what the lake bottom samples might reveal. We were also curious about each other's profession, and talked for at least twenty minutes. We talked about his trees. We talked about West Michigan's geology and the area's oil and gas reserves. I told him that I preferred the life-sciences to the physical sciences and mentioned in jest that I found geology about as interesting as a box of rocks. He chuckled, and went into a long dissertation about why geology is important and fascinating.

His voice rose with excitement when I told him that I'd actually tried to see what the attraction was, and had read John McPhee's Pulitzer Prize winning, *Annals of the Former World*. It is a saga of the geological record of the United States at the 40th parallel. John McPhee is one of my favorite authors. He normally writes about subjects from the natural world, covering topics such as orange trees or the Pine Barrens in New Jersey. His book, *Encounters with the Archdruid,* is considered a classic. It's a record of the friendly, but often contentious dialogues between David Brower, past president of the Sierra Club, and three separate developers. The book is a revealing insight into the conflict between wilderness preservation and society's need for natural resources.

To my surprise, the geologist knew the famous author personally. He had worked down the hall from him when they both taught at a university out east. He said that John McPhee was more knowledgeable about geology than most geologists.

We eventually hung up, and, to my disappointment, I never heard from him again. I never learned whether or not the students used one of his trees. It is one of the drawbacks to my job. If I solve a client's problem or answer their question, it is not uncommon to never hear from them again.

✳

Sitting at the picnic table, dragging my feet about making breakfast, I closed my eyes to listen more closely to the distant surf and tipped my face upward to embrace the morning light. With my eyes closed, I can distinguish two separate sounds the lake is creating. There is the deeper rumble from the surf. The other sound, however, is quieter, yet closer. The bay in front of the campground where I'm staying is protected by outer islands. Gentler waves are swishing through the gravel beach fifty feet away. That beach gravel is clear evidence of how long waves have washed onto shore at Belle Isle—long enough to turn Precambrian basalt into pea-gravel, but not long enough to turn the pea-gravel into sand.

The geologist would tell me that Lake Superior is a very young lake. He'd tell me the most recent glaciers of the Wisconsin Age, which scooped out the basin for Lake Superior, receded only 10-to-15 thousand years ago. He'd tell me the fossil and smoothed-stone evidence of corals located at the higher elevations pre-date the "recent" ice age by millennia.

I wondered if the sediment data from Lake Michigan proved useful to the Great Lakes Institute. Their ecologists hoped the data would show them environmental trends. Those trends feel more like fads compared to the geological record that the rock strata at Isle Royale reveal. Isle Royale is founded upon some of the oldest rock on the planet. In fact, McPhee called the geology of the Great Lakes Region some of the most stable and "boring" in the country. What does 100 or 1,000 years matter when measured against billions? Even a million years into the future, will our industrial age and its reliance on hydrocarbons be detectable to future geologists? Will that mysterious slice of smudge in a soil profile be misinterpreted as an ancient forest fire instead of the leftover grit from smoke stacks?

I was recently given one of the island's most ancient stones—an Isle Royale greenstone. It was given to me by one of the few remaining island property owners. She gave me the marble-sized semi-precious stone as a gift when we disembarked from the ferry in Copper Harbor. On a previous trip to the island, we'd discussed the dilemma of her family's eventual loss of their beloved cabin. As part of the 1941 legislation that created Isle Royale National Park, all private land holdings were to be bequeathed to the National Park Service at fair market value no later than the third generation. Her Dad was that generation.

While we were crossing the lake, I asked her where I might acquire a greenstone. I needed to get one for a friend who'd asked me to buy him one while I was passing through the Keweenaw. He wanted to set the greenstone in a ring as a gift for his wife.

The greenstone, Chlorastrolite, is the official gemstone of the State of Michigan and found only at Isle Royale and on the Keweenaw Peninsula. Greenstones are a by-product of lava bubbles that perked to the surface during the formation of the area, which makes them incredibly old. Geologists say the Great Lakes Region hasn't perked or bubbled for over 1.2 billion years.

When she gave me the stone, I was overwhelmed by her kindness and momentarily speechless. When I found my voice, I explained that I hadn't been implying she give me one of hers. But she insisted that I take it, asking that in exchange I talk to the Park Service about her family's plight, which I did. (Sadly, there's little hope their cabin will survive. Very few cabins will be retained, and those strictly for historical preservation's sake.)

When I returned home, I balked at giving the greenstone to the friend who'd asked for it. Chris is a fellow arborist at the tree service and he, too, had gone to college at Michigan Tech, which is located in the Keweenaw Peninsula. The greenstone, besides being a gift for his wife, would also be a reminder of his three-year stay in northern Michigan.

I didn't give him the gem for a long time.

It was a greenstone, after all. I didn't own any. It represents Isle Royale. The deep aqua-green, smoky hues remind me of the island's conifer-flanked hills. The silver-laced sparks within the stone brought to mind the glint of the sun's rays reflected off Lake Superior. The tiny stone spoke of the island before lichen dotted the landscape, before the island lay buried beneath thousands of feet of ice, before it lay beneath an ancient inland sea. Not to mention, the dusty little stone—it hadn't been polished yet—was given to me!

Gandalf would have been proud. With great reluctance I held to my original purpose and gave up the stone, beginning to understand some people's fascination for geology. Rocks lock down time, and if I could place the very essence of Isle Royale into a seed of stone, a greenstone would be my choice.

Six months later, his wife showed me how the ring turned out, and with a heavy sigh, I told her, "It's beautiful."

In comparison to rocks, for us humans, time streaks by. Taking another sip of coffee, it occurred to me that my month here was nearing an end. Yet, on the up side, after fifty years of living on this planet, I had finally taken some time to do nothing more than explore. And "taking time" is the right expression for it. Nobody gives you time to do such ventures.

I hadn't come to Isle Royale to find purpose or the meaning of life. When I was all alone at night, staring into the depths of the Milky Way, and worshiping a God who creates such wonders, I'd been more than content to just … be.

The sabbatical was meant to be a time to rest, time to enjoy each day, a time to explore.

To notice that red squirrels glean seeds from spruce cones in nice neat rows as if eating corn on the cob. To watch the sun rise, to watch it emerge from Lake Superior, climb the eastern sky and spread its light down the opposite hillside. To see sunlight travel through a birch tree, and splash the forest floor with speckled quivers. To listen to the music of the wind …

To distinguish the flutter of an aspen leaf from a maple, the whisper of spruce needles versus pine …

To paddle lakes I'd never paddled, to hike off-trail, to touch trees … to consider the lifecycle of the spruce adelgid … to come to grips with what happened to all of the ash … to question how a giant pine manages to thrive with so little soil …

The lessons Dad taught me.

Ken's dedication to his father.

My mentor's teaching, his reminder that ignorance is not bliss.

It will be hard to leave this place. But I miss my wife and my sons. I miss hearing about their day. I confess to also wanting to brag to friends about surviving in the wild for an entire month. And to take a hot shower would be nice.

Normally, at sunrise, I turn my thoughts toward what lies ahead—what places I want to see, what fishing lures to use, what chores need to be done. I'd be preparing for another day of island living. Sunsets—it seems to me, not sunrises—are the time to look back and grow introspective.

This morning, however, as I finished my cup of coffee, the sunrise causes me to look back … and ahead. Between the sifting of the waves through the gravel like clockwork and the beginning of another day, I'm once again feeling I have a deadline. Time, once again, presses me.

No less than Steven Hawking wrote that time requires motion and that without something moving—a clock-hand, a speeding car, the revolution of the earth around the sun—time would in essence stand still. The poets use motion as a metaphor for time—a river's flow, or the ebb and fall of the tides, the passing of the seasons.

Isle Royale has its own way of measuring time. And in only one month, I'd adopted "Island Standard Time." Each wave's tumble represents one second. The time it takes for a gust of wind to sweep across Robinson Bay represents a minute. The time it takes for a moose to swim across Lane Cove represents an hour. Sunrises and sunsets mark each day, and the years can be counted in the trees by each whorl of limbs on the conifers.

Yet, it is really Lake Superior that sets the pace here. You can't reach this island without spending hours crossing its waters, and Superior's waves beat upon the island so constantly that after a couple of days you barely notice the sound anymore. It's not until the wind dies and the lake grows still that you notice its absence. There is a palpable hush. A sense that time has stopped. But it's deceptive.

Not to argue with the likes of Hawking, but when the wind dies, and the lake calms, and the trees go still, time does not stop. Instead the universe is simply beckoning our attention.

The island tenses at such moments. The lake poises, preparing itself for some change. It neither feels peaceful nor calm. The silence begs the question. What's next?

FAREWELL

"Dreams come true. Without that possibility,
nature would not incite us to have them.

~John Updike

TONIGHT, MY DESTINATION IS THE OPEN LAKE. I WILL CANOE NORTH AND WHEN I reach median lake depth, which is 483 feet, I'll set the paddle down, slide into my sleeping bag, and try to sleep. I don't have far to go. Three miles north of the island, the lake is already over 500-feet deep.

The forecast calls for calm-to-one-footers, with light and variable winds. Skies are expected to remain clear. But I carry a battery-powered hand-held marine radio so as not to be surprised by a sudden change. Marine forecasts are given around the clock, and the monotone voices of the NOAA announcers relay nothing but facts. The Canadian forecasters out of Thunder Bay betray no emotion and are refreshingly undramatic compared to the weather people I normally listen to in the States. Even gale warnings are given as if reading a business report. More importantly, the forecasts are reliably accurate.

Passing through the gap between Captain Kidd and Amygdaloid Islands, I stop paddling for a moment to look back at Isle Royale. The island is dark. There are no cabin lights or campfires to be seen. An inky silhouette of jagged tree tops rim the southern skyline, punching holes in the Milky Way. The night's dew atomizes the forest's exhalations. Even from a couple of miles out, the air has a resin-rich aroma. I instantly picture dark pines where moose sleep lightly, while wolves hunt.

There's no moon, and yet the sky is amazingly bright overhead. As predicted, the lake is calm, but not stone-still and, the surface of the water acts like a warped mirror. When I dip the paddle into that pool of reflected lights, the stars glint, crinkle and waver as if they're too delicate to touch. Within six feet of the canoe, the stars' reflections off the lake are fairly sharp, almost pinpoint, but not quite. Past six feet, the stars begin to blur, and beyond that, their reflections merge and give the surface of the lake a dull sheen. It's an eerie sort of light, as if Superior's holding secrets.

Once past the protection of the outer islands, I begin to feel a slight rhythmic lift to the canoe. The Smoker Craft slopes upward and then downward on the rollers, gently rocking forward and aft. Ducks explode into flight and my heart does the proverbial leap into my throat. I'm sure they surprised me more than I did them. They are fast. The beat of their strong wings and quick retreat sounds for no more than a couple of seconds. Did they mistake me for a giant otter?

I pick up the paddle and continue my journey.

An hour later, I stop and set the paddle beneath the seat. The canoe glides to a stop. The ripples from my wake fade and disappear. The surface of the lake looks like white-speckled black silk.

Tonight, I will say my thanks.

If possible, which it isn't, I hope to adequately thank God for my family, for letting me make it to age 50, for the life I've had, for my time on Isle Royale, and for whatever lies ahead. I will be entrusting whatever future I have into His hands.

Tonight's paddle is also a celebration. And there's something about a sky full of stars that makes me feel like I'm at a party. The stars seem happy to see me tonight.

Searching the horizon, I see two lighthouses blinking. One is at Passage Island, four miles off the northeast tip of Isle Royale. The other light is from Canada. There is an ore freighter visible to the west, probably heading for Thunder Bay to pick up more wheat or pulpwood. The freighter must be a long way away because I don't hear it. On quiet nights, the deep throb of their engines can be heard as far as 20 miles. I don't hear any jets overhead either, but see two pairs of red and green blinking lights moving across the southwest sky.

To the east, Lake Superior extends 250 miles before it finds the far shore. There's no sign of man-made objects in that direction. There are no ships, no planes in the sky; not even a lighthouse can be seen. It occurs to me that I am observing a span of water that's over 100 square miles in size.

I am doing my best not to think about the fathoms that lie below. The lake is a giantess I'd prefer pays me no attention.

I need to somehow silence my thoughts this evening. Thoughts can be deafening. I've tried similar ventures before with mixed results. This night, however, I want to silence that incessant mental dialogue. A sleeping pad and sleeping bag are rolled up together and tied to the bottom of a spar to keep them off the floor of the canoe. Every time I cross over to paddle on the other side, the paddle drips water into the canoe. I brought an extra shirt to soak up the water before I spread out the bedroll.

Despite the calm lake conditions, there's a surprising amount of sound, mostly soft gurgles and plinks, and my slightest movement or squirm causes the canoe to creak. Being perfectly still is difficult to do. But when I manage it, there is a background of silence. Silence has implications. There's a vastness to it. I don't hear any cars in the distance and there's no boat traffic on the lake. No voices carry across the water. No cabin doors slam. No dishes rattle or music plays through screened windows—none of those well-inhabited, inland lake sounds I'm accustomed to hearing back home.

Another hour passes and what little wind there was has now dropped off. The lake glasses-over, a rare event. The stars' reflections clarify.

I sponge up what little water has splashed into the canoe and spread my bedroll out. I carefully slide into the bag and lay still, trying to respect the silence. It's so quiet now that I can hear my heart beating. The hull may be amplifying its thumps, and I wonder if my heart is causing ripples on the water.

I lay back, arms at my sides, and stare up at the stars. My eyes begin to grow heavy and I yawn. I tell the stars I'm tired now.

The lake cradles me in my canoe.

I drop into a dreamless sleep.

AFTERWORD / ACKNOWLEDGEMENTS

The canoe is gone. She finally made her escape … but not until we'd retired her. Ken and I had reached the conclusion, some years ago now, that the Smoker Craft was no longer sea worthy. She was making so many squeaks and groans and complaints that we just couldn't ignore them any longer. We had legitimate fears she'd sink beneath us or split in two during one of our dashes across a bay or cove.

The Smoker Craft certainly didn't owe us anything. The canoe had more than served us well, as she'd served all her previous owners. I'd bought the canoe for a mere fifty bucks from my brother-in-law, Brian. That would be the same Brian Engman who worked on the island on a trail crew in the 1980s and kayaked home across Lake Superior. When Brian sold me the canoe, (it was pretty beat-up even then) he said he'd bought it from someone else, who had bought it from someone before him. Who exactly bought the canoe originally nobody remembers.

Given the canoe's long and illustrious career, and given its declining condition, Ken and I thought about holding a retirement party for her, which sounds noble, at first. The ceremony, however, entailed drilling holes in the aluminum hull and bequeathing her to the depths of Lake Superior during one of the Isle Royale Queen's lake crossings. Captain Don, knowing something of the canoe's rich history, was agreeable to the task. The fact that he and his crew had more than once hauled its bulk onto the top of the ship for transport to the island may have had some bearing on his decision.

In the end, however, we couldn't do it. Cooler heads prevailed, or at least more pragmatic heads, and we decided to keep the Smoker Craft for small ventures on small waters, at least far smaller than on Lake Superior. We decided to store the old canoe either at my son's place in Hancock or at my summer home near Dollar Bay, and she did see some use.

On occasion, we'd take her fishing on Portage Lake or drive her up to Gratiot Lake to catch some walleye. I thought the Smoker Craft was enjoying a nice leisurely retirement, one in fact that I rather envied. Retiring to the North Country, fishing whenever I felt like it, and resting between ventures at a cottage in the woods sounds pretty nice. A couple years ago, my son asked if he could stash the Smoker Craft beside a remote Upper Peninsula lake for the fall. It's a lake that you can only reach on foot. Stashing the canoe there, he said, would avoid portaging all 70 pounds of it back and forth over the mile-long path. The small lake was a secret fishing hole of his, and he assured me the lake was no bigger than a large pond. So I agreed to the move with a reminder not to trust her too much.

Unfortunately, before my son could carry out his plan, he had a big split-up with his girlfriend who sold the Smoker Craft along with several of his other worldly possessions before he could rescue them. Despite his pleas, she was unwilling to tell us the canoe's new owner.

So ... the canoe has moved on.

Much like the canoe's career, this book, too, has weathered a storm or two. It has been almost fifteen years since I spent the month on Isle Royale, and a lot of water has slid beneath me, as well. To properly explain the delay for finishing the second Isle Royale book, a little back-tracking is in order. During that month-long sojourn in 2002, I wrote two drafts for two separate books. One of them would become *Naked in the Stream: Isle Royale Stories*, which attempts to capture our thirty years of Isle Royale trips, and is told from the perspective of an outdoor enthusiast. Each true story was selected to describe what it was like to vacation there, including the two stories that didn't directly involve Ken and I – "The Crossing" and "Off Shore Wind."

As is obvious by now, the second book, *Hidden in the Trees: An Isle Royale Sojourn*, is not exactly a sequel. The first book was meant to share our adventures. This second book is meant to describe Isle Royale through the eyes of an arborist. Caring for trees for a living has had a tremendous effect on how I view nature, and thus a tremendous effect on how I see wilderness. Spending an entire month on Isle Royale emphasized how polar-opposite the two natural worlds are—the urban landscape I work with at home, the other, a wilderness island. The difference between the two landscapes is so great that there were times when it was painful to see.

Southwest Michigan, as well as most of the Midwest, will never again be the same place it was before the Europeans arrived. The changes to the land and to the water are too great. Even the experts can't predict what the region would evolve into if left alone. Isle Royale, on the other hand, has been left to its own devices for eighty-plus-years. Isolated as Isle Royale is, and protected as it is, there is a feel, a scent, an authenticity to the island that really can't be adequately described. To fully appreciate such a place, you need to experience it firsthand. I was extremely fortunate to do just that.

That we have a place on this planet where direct human intervention is forbidden (except for the possible upcoming introduction of wolves) isn't just extraordinary, it's close to unbelievable. Such places are few and far between. I now understand why the U.N. designated Isle Royale a World Biosphere Preserve.

Part of the reason for the delay for *Hidden in the Trees, An Isle Royale Sojourn* is that I still work at the tree service, and they've been busy years.

When it comes to urging this book onward, nobody was a bigger "urger" than Susan Bays, publisher at Arbutus Press. I also have Susan to thank for taking the book to "summer camp" as she called her publishing company, then tell me, "Don't worry. We'll take good care of your child." Thank you, Susan.

Joyce Koskenmaki's artwork speaks for itself. Our initial meeting was also the result of Susan's prompts. Susan had seen some of Joyce's artwork, noted she'd served as Artist-in-Residence at Isle Royale National Park, and asked me to stop by Joyce's studio to talk with her about our project. We had a pleasant conversation over coffee and I handed her the manuscript for review.

She called me the very next day, saying she'd read the manuscript through the night and couldn't put it down. "What do you want me to do?" she asked.

Thrilled, I replied, "I have no idea."

She chuckled and said she'd send me some samples. Since then, we've enjoyed the kind of artistic collaboration I could never have imagined. She is one of the kindest, most soft-spoken people I know. I count her as a dear friend.

Then there is Michael Zuidema. Mike's a former sports writer for the Grand Rapids Press, and Mike helped me to stay focused on what's important. I had always thought of this book as primarily being about trees and about Isle Royale. Mike, however, showed me that Hidden in the Trees may be about trees. It may be about Isle Royale, but always, always ... "Keep it personal. What readers want to know," he insisted, "is how they both affect you."

Phillip Sterling made some final and crucial adjustments to the manuscript with his grammatical and word-choice suggestions. An accomplished poet, Fulbright scholar, and retired college English professor – once again, this tree guy felt fortunate to work with such talented people.

Without the West Michigan Writer's Workshop, neither book would have ever seen the light of day. The group's assistance cannot be emphasized enough. As fellow writers, the group knew when I needed a gentle prod or a firm "That will never work" suggestion. Their diligence at making each word count has greatly influenced both books.

To Steve Beckwith, Albert Bell, Dan Johnson, Jane Griffeon, to Paul and Pat, to Lisa and Lisa, to Sarah and Sheila, to Fred and Norma and Nathan, as well as Bill and Dawn and Michael and Jonathon, and to the late Roger Meyer, I owe a debt of gratitude.

Mr. Steve Beckwith and Professor Albert Bell, who serve as the writers' group' coordinators simply will not allow you to slip into mere journaling.

I also wish to express my gratitude to the people I work alongside of at West Michigan Tree Services. To Susie Hines, to Philomena, Amy, Shirlene, Bob, to my bosses Dan and Larry who allowed me to take the month off paid, no less. To Chris and Nick and Dan and, over the years, at least fifty other wonderful tree people; you haven't just influenced my career, you've influenced the person I am today, how I see the natural world and care for the people we serve. They work at one of the most dangerous professions in the world. Their labors, sweat, and sometimes blood flow through the pages of this book.

I had the technical support of Mr. Lee Mueller, a fellow arborist and friend who works for the Davey Tree Expert Company. He made a few corrections that would have been most embarrassing had they not been discovered by him.

Dr. Deb McCullough at Michigan State University was of great assistance with the chapters on the emerald ash borer crisis. Her recollections of those early days and of our struggles to stop the pest were invaluable. John Bedford, with the Michigan Departments of Agriculture and Rural Development, shared his early EAB scouting experiences with me and helped to paint a clearer picture of those early days as well.

There are several island people who contributed their time and knowledge. They sat down for interviews and provided several important documents. Dorothy Stegman – who is the last living person to overwinter on the island – lent a personal input into the island's human history and a real flesh and blood context to Isle Royale's past.

Greatly appreciated is the continued efforts of Dr. Rolf Peterson and his wife Candy, and Dr. John Vucetich and his wife Leah. Their continued vital research of the wolf-moose relationship certainly augments what we know about the complex relationship between predators and their prey, whether they be wolves and moose or between an aphid and a ladybug.

Dr. Paul Brown also helped with the complicated task of differentiating how the Park Service deals with the park's two missions – that of protecting the wilderness, the other of preserving the island's human history.

Kristine L. Bradof, Executive Director for the Isle Royale & Keweenaw Parks Association has been a tremendous moral support for this book, not to mention adding a few minor corrections that were not so minor. Her "When is that next book coming," was also nice to hear. Excerpts of the book were also published in *Tree Services Magazine*, the *Michigan Landscape Magazine,* and *Michigan Blue Magazine*. Thank you to their editors, Rob Meyer, Amy Frankmann, and Howard Meyerson.

Finally … to Ken Glupker, what can I say? Not only would these books not be possible without you. I'd very likely never have set foot on the island. I'd never have caught the fish we did. I'd never have done half the ventures we've shared. Between best friends, little needs to be said. Actions speak louder than words, even when placed into books. Your actions, my friend, speak loud and clear.

To my sons … and to my beautiful wife and life partner, and the strongest person I know … hugs.

BIBLIOGRAPHY

After Johnson & Lyon, 1991. *Life Cycle of Cooley spruce gall adelgid,* The University of Arizona Cooperative Extension.

A Guide to the Plant Health Care Management System, Second Edition. International Society of Arboriculture, 1995.

Allen, Durward L. *Wolves of Minong, Isle Royale's Wild Community.* The University of Michigan Press, 1979.

Baldwin, Amalia Tholen. *Becoming Wilderness; Nature, History, and the Making of Isle Royale National Park.* Isle Royale and Keweenaw Parks Association, 2011.

Bell, Rob. *Velvet Elvis.* Zondervan, Grand Rapids, Michigan. 2005

BOREALIS, An Isle Royale Potpourri. Isle Royale Natural History Association, 1992.

Bronstein, Daniel A. *Law for the Expert Witness, second edition.* CRC Press, LLC, 1999.

Bryson, Bill. *A Short History of Nearly Everything.* Broadway Books, New York.

Building with Trees. The Arbor Day Institute, 1992.

Building with Trees. The National Arbor Day Foundation, 1995.

Burnham, Robert Jr. *Burnham's Celestal Handbook.* Dover Publications, Inc., 1978.

Carroll, Chris. *Hubble's Eye on Infinity.* National Geographic, December, 2003

Cleland, Charles E. *Rites of Conquest, The History and Culture of Michigan's Native Americans.* The University of Michigan Press, 1992.

Clifton, James A. & Cornell, George L. & McClurken, James M. *People of the Three Fires, The Ottawa, Potawatomi, and Ojibway of Michigan.* The Michigan Indian Press Grand Rapids Inter-Tribal Council, 1986.

Cochrane, Timothy. *Minong—The Good Place, Ojibwe and Isle Royale.* Michigan State University Press, 2009.

Cooper, Christopher. *Eyewitness Science Matter.* Dorling Kindersley Inc. 1992

Dillard, Annie. *Pilgrim at Tinker Creek.* HarperCollins, 1974.

Ecological Studies of Wolves on Isle Royale, 2001 – 2002. Annual Report 2001 – 2002 by Rolf O. Peterson & John A. Vucetich, School of Forestry and Wood Products Michigan Technological University, Houghton, Michigan, 2002.

Engelbert, Phyllis & Dupuis, Diane, L. *The Handy Space Answer Book.* Visible Ink Press, Detroit, MI., 1998.

Feynman, Richard P. *The Pleasure of Finding Things Out.* Michelle and Carl Feynman, 1999. Originally published by Perseus Publishing.

Gale, Thomas P. & Gale, Kendra L. *Isle Royale, A Photographic History.* Isle Royale History Association, 1995.

Glime, Janice M. *The Elfin World of Mosses and Liverworts of Michigan's Upper Peninsula and Isle Royale.* Isle Royale Natural History Association, 1993.

Gostomski, Ted & Marr, Janet. *Island Life, An Isle Royale Nature Guide.* Isle Royale Natural History Association, 2007.

Green, Brian. *The elegant universe: superstrings, hidden dimensions, and the quest for the ultimate theory.* W.W. Norton & Company, Inc. New York, N.Y. 10110
Gribbin, John. *Unveiling The Edge Of Time.* Harmony Books, New York, 1992

Hirshfeld, Alan, W. *Parallax, The Race to Measure the Cosmos.* W.H. Freeman and Company, 2001.

Johnson, Warren T. Lyon, Howard H. *INSECTS THAT FEED ON TREES AND SHRUBS,* Second Edition Revised. Cornell University, Ithaca and London, 1991.

Kohl, Johann Georg. *Kitchi-Gami, Life Among the Lake Superior Ojibway.* Minnesota Historical Society Press, 1985. Originally published by Chapman & Hall, 1860.

Kolb, Rocky. *Blind Watchers of the Sky.* Helix Books, Addison-Wesley Publishing Company. 1996.

McPhee, John. *Annals of the Former World.* Farrar, Strauss, & Giroux, 1981.

Michigan Forests. Michigan Department of Natural Resources Forest Management Division.

Minnesota Sea Grant, Minnesota Department of Resources

The Morton Arboretum. *The Landscape Below Ground: Proceedings of an International Workshop on Tree Root Development in Urban Soils.* Edited by Dr. Gary W. Watson, Dr. Dan Neely, Publication of The International Society of Arboriculture, Savoy, Ill. 1994.

Oikarinen, Peter. *Island Folk, The People of Isle Royale.* University of Minnesota Press, 2008. Originally published by the Isle Royale Natural History Association, 1979.

Parrat, Smitty & Welker, Doug. *The Place Names of Isle Royale.* Isle Royale Natural History Association, 1999.

Persig, Robert. *Zen and the Art of Motorcycle Maintenance.* HarperCollins, 1974.
Peterson, Rolf O. *The Wolves of Isle Royale, A Broken Balance.* Willow Creek Press, 1995.
2007.

Peterson, Carolyn C. *A View from the Wolf's Eye.* Isle Royale History Association, 2008.

Poirier, Jessica J. & Taylor, Richard E. *Images of America, Isle Royale.* Arcadia Publishing.

Smith, Norman F. *Trees of Michigan And The Upper Great Lakes, 6th Edition,* Thunder Bay Press, Lansing, Michigan. May, 1997

Rennicke, Jeff. *Isle Royale, Moods, Magic, & Mystique.* Isle Royale Natural History Association Houghton, Michigan.

Seglem, Elling. *Diaries of an Isle Royale Fisherman.* Isle Royale Natural History Association, 2002.

Service, Robert. *The Best of Robert Service.* Dodd, Mead & Company, Inc. Apollo Editions. 1953.

Shigo, A.L. *A New Tree Biology,* Durham, New Hampshire, 1986.

Shigo, A.L. *Tree Pruning. A worldwide Photo Guide.* Durham, New Hampshire, 1989.

Silvertson, Howard. *Once Upon An Isle, The Story of Fishing Families on Isle Royale.* Wisconsin Folk Museum, Inc. 1992.

Sockman, Ralph O. Famous quotes. Readers Digest, 1998.

Stegman, Nancy (Johnson). *Chippewa Harbor, Isle Royale National Park Michigan, Visitor Guide.*

The Isle Royale Institute, Fostering science and education of Isle Royale and the waters of Lake Superior. School of Forest Resources and Environment Sciences, Ecosystem Science Center, Houghton, Michigan.

Tolle, Eckhart. *The Power of Now, A Guide to Spiritual Enlightenment.* New World Library, 1997

Vergano, Dan. *Universe, knowledge expand.* USA TODAY, December 23, 2003

Vucetich, John A. *Winter Study 2011, Notes from the Field.*

ABOUT THE ARTIST

JOYCE KOSKENMAKI

Joyce Koskenmaki's drawings and paintings have been shown nationally and internationally. She has received many grants and awards and has taught at six different colleges and universities. She now lives in the Upper Peninsula of Michigan, near the forests of her childhood.

She walks in the woods every day, surrounded by the trees which are a constant presence in her work, both as subject and metaphor: she sees them as companions and protectors.

She has been an artist in residence at Isle Royale and has returned numerous times. Joyce provided illustrations for Vic Foerster's book, *Naked in the Stream, Isle Royale Stories*, published in 2010 by the Arbutus Press. Her website is www.joycekoskenmaki.com

Her painting on the cover of *Hidden in the Trees: An Isle Royale Sojourn* is titled *Rauha* which means peace in Finnish. It is oil on linen, about 30x30"

ABOUT THE AUTHOR

VIC FOERSTER

Vic wrote his classic account of experiences on Isle Royale National Park in *Naked In the Stream: Isle Royale Stories* in 2010. He had visited the park for thirty years with his camping pal, Ken.

Hidden in the Trees: An Isle Royale Sojourn, his sequel, encompasses more stories from the least visited National Park in the lower forty-eight states and also includes his keen observations about the natural world on the mainland as well.

As a certified arborist, Vic encorporates his experiences in the field with an eye toward philosophy and human intervention with nature's life-cycles. He looks at tree growth, injury, pests, disease and the final death of some of nature's finest gifts. He quotes poets, ponders grand ideas, and deals with breath-taking tree diseases. He recalls his experience as an expert in a court room trial, and his humbling encounters with tree customers overcome with loss and misunderstanding.

Once again, Vic's gift of looking at nature, at humans, at the grand design and intertwining it all in his writing brings readers to the woods to see through his eyes.

An Excerpt from *Naked in the Stream* by Vic Foerster

The Prologue

"STANDING AT THE PROW, I FACED FORWARD INTO THE WIND AND BREATHED. THE steel hull of the passenger ferry sliced through the lake, curling the gentle seas into two bow waves breaking on either side of the ship. At twelve knots, my eyes watered. Accustomed to pulling my way through the water with a paddle, the speed seemed reckless.

It was a relief to feel Lake Superior air on my face again. After spending a week outdoors, camping, I needed to get out of the pilothouse where I'd been catching up with Captain Don. Canoeing the past seven days and sleeping outside every night made me conscious of the slightest indoor sensation. Although Don had the doors wide open, the cabin still felt stuffy.

Only three other passengers were on the forward deck at the prow. It offered no protection from the cold breeze. People came and went quickly. We were two hours into the four-and-one-half hour boat ride from Isle Royale to Copper Harbor, and by now, the campers had scattered across the ship, each of them settled into a seat to their liking. Returning to the Michigan mainland, their vacations now over, everyone had that look on their face they get when they're reliving the past. There were only one-to-two footers on the lake. It was going to be a smooth ride today. Several passengers were sleeping. I walked over and stood alongside a young man leaning against the outside rail. With his elbows propped on the railing, he was staring out at the lake. He glanced over, smiled, and nodded. When I was in the pilothouse, I noticed him because he remained on the front deck, not leaving his vigilant study of the lake to find a cozier spot inside.

"How are you doing?" I asked, leaning forward against the rail next to him.

He didn't say anything for so long that I wondered if I heard. But then he said without turning to look at me, "You know ... I feel ... absolutely ... wonderful. This was my first trip to Isle Royale ... and ... I can't begin to say how great it was ... to get so far away. It's so ... quiet." His voice trailed away with the word "quiet" as if he was reluctant to speak too loudly. He then slowly turned, looked squarely into my face and asked, "How many times have you been to Isle Royale?"

His question surprised me, and it shouldn't have. It's a common question among passengers on the *Isle Royale Queen*. It's one of those icebreakers campers use when they meet someone they've never met before. But I hadn't thought about it for a long while. At my hesitation, he looked at me even more intently.

"I'm not sure," I said.

"Really?"

"Well, I've been coming almost every year for thirty years and sometimes more than once a year. I suppose it depends on how you count."

He seemed to have a hard time digesting that, so I added, "That's not a lot. Ken, my fishing partner, has been coming ten years longer than I, and of course, some people actually live and work out there."

He turned back to look at the lake again and said, "I can't imagine."

People get like that on Isle Royale. Separated from cars and traffic, TV and computers, their cell phones and all of the other accoutrements of civilization, returning to a more natural rhythm of living—it slows a person down. The wilderness island creates a more relaxed pace, makes me think about how I really feel about a matter before I jump into a conversation and squeeze my opinion into the frenetic discussions I so often have at home.

I found myself staring at him. He gazed back out at the water with a composed, relaxed expression, as if several years of hard living had recently melted away from such a young face. It struck me that he looked like me, only a me from thirty years ago.

Always eager to talk about Isle Royale, I proceeded to tell him about some of what I'd experienced over the years—close encounters with wolves and moose, the great fishing, sunrises over Lake Superior, and paddling across water so smooth the wake from the canoe was the largest ripple. But, after a few moments, I too became quiet. Maybe I sounded shallow. It felt like I was trying to impress him instead of sharing the experience, which he was so clearly reliving at that moment. It was as if I was showing him around my trophy room or talking about my trips to the island like each one was another notch on my adventure belt. Shutting up, I wished him well, walked around the ship to the stern and rejoined Ken.

He was sitting outdoors on the stern deck where we normally stake ourselves for the voyage home, reading a book he'd started on the island. I sat down next to him and watched the ship's wake and prop wash, which stretched behind us for a couple of hundred feet before dissolving into the lake. I couldn't get the brief conversation or the passenger's demeanor out of my mind. He made me realize my attitude about Isle Royale had changed over the years. Actually, it was more than that. He made me see I will never again look at the island as he does right now. But there was a time ...